SEAN MICHAEL CRANE

PRISON
OF YOUR OWN

Break Free of Limitations and
Unlock Your True Potential

NOTES FROM THE AUTHOR

I have described these events that transformed my life based on my personal recollection. I have changed the names of certain individuals in order to respect their privacy while still maintaining the integrity of specific events I describe in this book.

ACKNOWLEDGEMENTS

I dedicate this book to my Uncle Mike who has been a shining light within my life since the day I was born. If it wasn't for his presence in my life I would not be the man I am today.

I would also like to acknowledge my beautiful wife Jessica and our amazing children Mason, Scarlett and Preston as well as all my wonderful family members who have supported me through every challenge I faced and never gave up on me. I would not be here today without all their love and support.

ABOUT THE AUTHOR

At the age of 23 I was sentenced to 7 years in prison for a crime I didn't commit. It was in my prison cell, for the first time in my life, I faced my demons and challenges head on. I was able to completely transform my entire life behind bars. My attitude, my mentality, and my daily routines were all adjusted and allowed me to create new outcomes and results within my life. My personal transformation and the steps I took while incarcerated is what I wish to share with anyone who feels lost or hopeless in their life right now. These life changing steps saved my life and freed me from addiction, negative thinking and living life carelessly. I want you to know that no matter what you go through deep within you is the capacity to persevere and create a life you love and cherish.

For me it was life or death! I had to make drastic changes if I were able to live the life I truly wanted. However, it wasn't one big change that took place over night. I spent every day, over 2,000 days, in prison cultivating the person I wanted to be. I created a process that allowed me to go from a drug addict with nothing to a husband & father, life coach, author, motivational speaker and ironman in less than 3 years. If I did this from a prison cell, with nothing, I promise you can take control of your life too! You deserve it and you are far more capable than you realize!

I am here to support you 100%

To learn more about this life changing process and the exact steps me and my clients have used to completely transform our lives visit seanmichaelcrane.com.

SEAN CRANE LIFE COACHING

I am on a mission to guide others through the same process that helped me transform my life so they can discover their true potential and create the life they have always envisioned.

First, we must uncover where your challenges and perceived limitations stem from so we can resolve them entirely before moving forward to create the life of your dreams. Otherwise it will always feel impossible or the changes we make will be temporary and we will revert back to our old ways.

I have a very specific, step by step process that I mastered while in prison and allowed me to transform my life from a small cell with nothing. This is the same approach that has helped other people just like you overcome their struggles and create fulfillment and purpose within their lives.

If you want to overcome your current challenges and achieve all your goals in the most direct route possible visit my website seanmichaelcrane.com for free resources and courses to help you start taking action to live a life you love and cherish.

MINDSET

Your mentality is everything and is the determining factor in whether or not you win or lose the daily battles that create your reality.

I teach my clients how to cultivate a winners mindset and achieve massive success in all areas of life using positive mindset hacks and other techniques that helped me thrive in the negative prison environment.

HEALTH & FITNESS

Creating energy and confidence through action is essential. My coaching program focuses on sustainable health and fitness routines that are custom built to help you maximize your results.

We will give you the tools you need to sculpt your dream physique and establish habits in both nutrition and fitness that will provide a lifetime of results.

LIFESTYLE

Your routines and habits are essential for success. I specialize in creating powerful personal routines that have the capacity to transform your life. My blueprint to success strategy ensures you have optimal balance between work and family life while still empowering you to achieve all your personal goals. When you consistently implement positive routines in your life you will create unwavering confidence within yourself, strengthen your relationships, and thrive in business without feeling overwhelmed and burnt out.

FEEL STUCK OR LOST BUT KNOW YOU WERE MADE FOR MORE? I AM HERE TO SUPPORT YOU

VISIT seanmichaelcrane.com

TESTIMONIALS

Thank you Sean Michael Crane for believing in me! I've grown so much since joining your program. At one point I contemplated ending my life. That's how low and hopeless I felt. I am now clean and sober, in the process of starting my own business with my new embroidery machine and I will be training to complete my first Ironman event in 2021. I now have the inner peace and self love I spent over a decade searching for and I'm so grateful to be taking action to become the man I want to be!

Diego Rivera, client & friend

I've known Sean over 15 years and recently reconnected for guidance to become a better version of me. He has helped me become what I've always envisioned to be as a father, a better partner but most important a better man.

Edgar Guerrero, client & friend

Sean refused to give up on me and believed that I could achieve my goals even when I was doubtful. I can't thank him enough for his support and motivation to help me get in the best shape of my life both mentally and physically.

Scott Gutentag, client & former school counselor

Sean's story and personal mentorship have helped shape and change my perspective, my mindset, my vision, and my life's trajectory. His powerful story and deep passion for helping people are truly inspiring and life-transforming.

Ben Presson, client & friend

To see this young man rise like a Phoenix from the ashes of his youth has been a life altering experience for me. Sean obviously learned hard lessons in jail that I pray I never have to personally experience and learn. The experience changed him forever and made him a champion among men and aged his soul in a way that most only experience after an entire lifetime of good and bad experiences. I'm not sure how I would have survived 2020 without him. Today I'm doing things I've never done before, I'm more active than I was in my 20's and I'm in my 50's. I take time daily for myself with a variety of routines and habits he helped me realize the value of. I have probably experienced more loss and grief in the last 5 years than all the years before that and I am more stable and happier than I have ever been. I'm not really sure how to explain how impactful what he did for me was other than to say it positively altered me forever.

Julie Koonce, client & family friend

Before working with Sean I was plagued with guilt and frustration over my past, and consumed with a future that hasn't happened yet. Through our work together, I have learned to reduce stress and be present in the moment, truly enjoying life for what it is. A blessing!

Shaun Fraley, client & friend

Sean's expertise and guidance was invaluable in helping me through a really hard time in my life. Working with Sean helped me develop the tools I needed to be a healthier person both physically and mentally.

Clayton Leasure, client & friend

As a husband, father of 3 teenagers and entrepreneur of 100 employees, I found every excuse not to take care of my mind, body and spirit. Working with Sean I have found a higher level of personal excellence in all three. Through his coaching and my daily routines, I'm becoming the person I've always wanted to be. Thank you Sean!

Will Hallett, client & friend

Working with Sean has been a game changer for me! I had lost direction. I lacked motivation and focus on where I was going and what I was doing with my life. In just a short time Sean helped me turn my entire life around. I'm now the person I used to be 10 years ago.

Diane Augustus, client & friend

TABLE OF CONTENTS

PRELUDE

I'll never forget the long walk to the prison yard. It was evening by the time I approached the lifeless cement structure—the mere sight of it stirring feelings of apprehension within. The barbed wire and manned gun towers lined the perimeter emphatically. It was surreal, to say the least, like something out of a novel or movie, a bad dream gone on too long. I was still in shock and disbelief. Taking it in, I felt like everything was in slow motion so I wouldn't miss the symbolism of the moment.

Each step felt like a hundred smaller steps, and a whirlwind of thoughts and emotions flooded my mind and body. As I walked closer, I played out different scenarios in my head. What would the next five years be like? What was I in for? What was going to happen? In those moments of doubt and fear, I experienced a life-altering shift in my perspective. One that would transform the way I viewed everything I experienced going forward.

I noticed, off in the distance beyond the barbed wire and intimidating buildings, the sun setting on the vast horizon. I'll never forget that moment, imprinted on my memory forever. As the sky turned purple, the sun looking massive, bigger than I'd ever seen it before, I felt a surge of energy, invigorating and palpable throughout my body.

I'd never seen a sunset of this magnitude. I was captivated. It was almost as if I were in a trance. I couldn't stop staring out at the evening sky and the contrast of vivid colors. I can't explain what was happening to me at that moment, but I could feel it. For the first time in a long time, I was paying attention. I was connected to the moment, and it was all I had. I was alive!

What I discovered while I was in prison was a gift, a secret, a miracle—and I wish to share it with you in this book. Every day while I was incarcerated, I would meditate and pray that one day I could share all these thoughts, feelings, and realizations from that time. Now that has become a reality. A mere thought became an unrelenting vision that I manifested into existence. And that is the secret I wish to share with you: you possess unlimited potential right now! And that potential can impact and transform every part of your life.

I want everyone who is reading this to know that you can change your life at any moment. No matter what you've been through and experienced, the ability to transform is deep within you. You already have everything it takes to create a life you love and cherish.

I hope my story inspires you to pursue your dreams and the feelings and desires that accompany such grand visions. Can you feel it? Like there's something there, deep within, that knows you're capable of more? That the thought of settling or missing out on your dreams terrifies you? Can you feel that inner greatness and your true and authentic self screaming to be unleashed? Don't ever lose hope, don't ever give up on those feelings and those desires, for they may help you through dark times, just as they did for me. They can lead you to the life you're destined to live. Don't hold back any longer; this is your time.

THE EARLY YEARS
MY CHILDHOOD

I grew up in what felt like paradise, fifteen minutes away from Santa Barbara, California, in my hometown of Goleta, a picture-perfect community tucked away on the coastline bordering the Pacific Ocean. It was probably one of the best places to grow up in the world. We had beaches, parks, sports leagues, family gatherings, neighborhood friends, and everything that felt safe and comforting.

My family dynamic was different but felt so special growing up. I was the oldest of three children. Since my dad was one of nine children, I had plenty of aunts, uncles, and cousins who lived close by. My dad's eldest brother, Uncle Mike, even lived with us as early as I can remember. He was fun, loving, and always smiling. To us kids, he was the best. From the earliest memories I have, we were always together. The adults would sit in the living room while the kids ran around the neighborhood or played in the backyard. Every day was an adventure and life felt exciting.

Family was everything in those days, and I remember everyone being close and connected. This was ingrained into me early on, and it felt like everyone was supportive and loyal to one another. Looking back, I realize these were the strongest beliefs instilled into my siblings and me. Family, loyalty, and unity. This was what mattered. We were all together, and that's the way it should be.

Prior to age ten, my life revolved around sports and family. I loved baseball, basketball, and football. I played all three sports every year, and when I wasn't playing, I was watching games on TV. This was my world. I dreamed of being a professional athlete, so every birthday, that's what I wished for when I blew out my candles.

In those early years, life seemed like such a gift. My dreams and the excitement I had felt magical. I lived in a world of endless possibilities and felt fully capable of carrying out my dreams and living a fulfilling life. Even at that early age, I always had a deep-rooted belief that I was destined to experience extraordinary things. Of course, I had no idea the trajectory my life would take in the coming years. When I look back and reflect, this is the most genuine and innocent version of myself that ever existed. I didn't hold back on anything I did, and I was infused with love, passion, and desire for life. This is who I am at my core. All the love I was exposed to by my family in my formative years affected my development in such a positive way that it cannot go unstated.

It wasn't until age ten that I recall thinking differently about my life or the world for that matter. Up until that point, I had been very sheltered and protected. Although I've heard stories that paint a different picture, my early life was wonderful. I didn't know the extent of my parents' struggles and was naive to the problems looming in our household. All I knew was that we had a big family that loved each other, and we all spent tons of time together.

There were incidents I can recall that clashed with the values of our loving family and the lens by which I viewed the world. I couldn't fully understand what was going on at that time and may have suppressed more than I realized. This was evident in a nightmare I would often have in which a silly and harmless cartoon background would be accompanied by the feeling of impending doom. In my dream, a timer ominously clicked faster and faster to an explosion. Every time the timer ran out, I would wake up terrified and out of breath. I couldn't make sense of it at that young age, but I hated it. I would tell my parents or Uncle Mike about my dream, but I don't think they understood how horrifying it was for me. I would often go find Uncle Mike and sleep in his bed on those nights. I gravitated toward him as a kid.

As far back as I can remember, he represented love, safety, and everything good in our world. But around age ten, I started to sense something, becoming increasingly anxious. I got into the habit of biting my nails and always felt concerned that something bad was going to happen.

I'm not sure where it stemmed from, but I slowly grew out of this nervous state. In retrospect, I believe it had to do with arguments or confrontations I witnessed growing up—possibly from some incidents I saw that were traumatic and difficult to process at a young age.

Despite all the love we felt, there was a dark side that we children were unaware of. It was always lurking below the facade of our pleasant upbringing. It was only a matter of time before we would experience things that were contrary to the comfortable life we had known. The nightmare I mentioned previously was more foreboding than I could have ever imagined.

The adults in my life early on were all loving people who wanted the best for me and the other children. Thank God for all my aunts and uncles. I was very fortunate to have so many loving people in my life—especially Uncle Mike who was the most amazing person I've ever met. He has shown me and my siblings unconditional love and support. It is because of his influence in my early life that I am the person I am today. Every ounce of good I possess was instilled by his presence and influence in my life.

My parents did their best and I know how much they loved me and my siblings. Yet, their personal issues took a tremendous toll on the family over time. I've gone back and forth as to how much I want to share about these times in my life. But since experiencing so much early on shaped my life forever and affected who I've become, I feel compelled to share these details. Otherwise, my message could be lost or less effective. I'm here to convey the truth as it was seen and felt from my perspective growing up. Now with the benefit of being removed from those times, I've come to peace with and accepted my past. I am not here to cast a negative light upon anyone; I merely want to describe the most impactful moments of my life, the ones that shaped who I am today.

My parents, despite their intentions, were struggling with a drug and alcohol addiction. As a young kid, I loved my parents dearly and they always showed my siblings and me love in return. However, from as early as I can remember, I knew something was different about them. Kids are intuitive and pick up on things adults don't always realize. At the time, I didn't know exactly what was different, but I was keenly aware that my parents were not the same as my friends' parents or my aunts and uncles. As I got older, their addictions became worse, and I became more aware of what was going on. Thankfully Uncle Mike was living with us, acting as head of the house and doing his best to provide security and feelings of normalcy for us. However, he couldn't shelter us entirely. I have images and specific memories that are still with me today, painfully etched in my consciousness forever.

I loved my parents very much and tried to ignore the nagging feelings I had about them. I was confused and sad because I couldn't understand their struggles, and I just wanted to have the same kind of parents everyone around me had. For the longest time, I held on to the delusion that my siblings and I could have a normal upbringing, whatever that meant.

It wasn't all bad, though. We had a lot of good times together. It just appears in retrospect that the dark times always overshadowed any good times we experienced.

My father was a very kind and compassionate man. I must have been eight or nine at the time I recall him most fondly. He would always be there after school to walk my sister and me home. He was a cheerful man, always charming and polite with my teachers and other parents.

I vividly remember my father and I taking walks at night with the family dog. It was really the only time the two of us would be alone and just talk. I didn't fully understand at the time, but I recall alcohol always being taboo, and sometimes he would tell me he was going to quit drinking. This would usually come the day after an argument at home. At the time, I didn't really understand why he was telling me this or what he was trying to say, but looking back, I think my dad had a lot of unresolved issues in his life and he probably didn't have anyone to talk to about them.

The arguments at home weren't common in those days. They typically occurred while my siblings and I slept, but when I could hear them, they scared me.

Although my mother was loving and affectionate, I can recall noticing something different in her from an early age. She seemed to be lost in thought often, as if she was daydreaming. It was like she was longing for something different while she was taking care of my siblings and me. Prior to age ten, I remember having loving interactions with my parents and feeling happy. But as the oldest, I also felt a sense of responsibility and, with age, became more aware of the burden that entailed.

Scary or unnerving events became more frequent, and they affected me a lot. When arguments or scary situations were unfolding, I would feel a paralyzing fear inside. I hated that feeling and would bite my nails in an attempt to distract myself. It never worked. I was just left with bleeding fingertips and the same unresolved emotions that caused the behavior in the first place. I had heard arguments late at night amongst the adults but we kids never saw anything traumatic for along. However, that changed the first time I saw my mother overdose. Panic and fear stained the air. It was suddenly silent; no one was speaking. I knew something was horribly wrong. As I walked back to my parents' bedroom, I saw my mom on the ground unconscious, and Uncle Mike was giving her mouth-to-mouth.

The next thing I remember was being in a room with my sister, Sara, and my brother, Kevin, away from whatever was going on. It all happened very fast and the details of that day are somewhat blurry.

The next memory I have is of my mom coming in the front door later that evening with an embarrassed look on her face. She was hugging Uncle Mike and crying. I could feel the energy from all that emotion. I didn't know what to make of it all; I just knew everyone's behavior was odd. My dad told us that my mother had fainted and she was better now. I still have the image of her on the bedroom floor unconscious vividly imprinted in my memory. Those are the things children never forget.

Unfortunately, it wasn't the last time this happened. The second time my mother overdosed, I was a little older, maybe eleven or twelve. I distinctly remember taking my brother and sister into my bedroom and trying to distract them. All the while, I had this paralyzing feeling seize my body. This time I was terrified, more aware of my mother's precarious condition. The ambulance arrived and we watched as she was taken away. While my mother would be okay, the effects of this particular incident scarred me. I was traumatized, although I may have not appeared so at the time. A short time after this incident, Uncle Mike and I were driving home from baseball practice and an ambulance pulled out in front of us as we neared our house. I felt a pang of dread consume my entire body, scared that the ambulance would be going to our house. Every turn the ambulance stayed ahead of us, my concern mounted. I was terrified. At the last minute, the ambulance headed in a different direction, and I was finally able to breathe. The fear of my mother dying was on my mind often in those days. She would overdose several more times while I was a kid, and each time, it felt like part of my heart was crushed. Years later, I would recount this story to my mother with tears pouring down my face. It was the first time I had ever talked about it with anyone. Over the years, I held so much emotion inside. I did not dare express it and acknowledge those horrible memories.

I always felt I had to be strong, stoic, and brave for my younger siblings. It was my responsibility to protect them. This mentality became a part of my identity, and I often felt like I was more responsible than my parents. No one told me I had to take on this role, but I did, possibly what felt like out of necessity. I felt a constant pressure and burden upon me. Despite appearing strong and courageous on the outside, I had to fight a raging battle inside of me for many years.

The wonderful times of my childhood, filled with love and joy sharply contrast with the memories that depict a much darker reality, where fear and despair plagued our lives. This symbolic theme has been a part of my life since inception. Over the years, I've seen it unfold in countless life experiences. Always present, below the surface, as if deep within the fabric of my being, good and evil energies reside in perpetual battle.

During my first month in high school, my life changed forever, as if a slow wick that had been burning since the day I was born had finally come to an end. In hindsight, it is apparent that it was only a matter of time before something devastating would happen within our family, but I don't think anyone could have anticipated the implosion that took place on this particular night. I recall the night vividly. I was fourteen, still very carefree and innocent. I was still more of a kid than anything and in my naivete, I wasn't prepared for what was about to transpire.

My dad was drunk—more so than I'd ever seen him before. He was arguing with Uncle Mike about something trivial. (When he drank, my dad would make a small situation into a catastrophe.) He called me back to his room and that's when I saw the gun in his hand. Fear shot through my body.

On this night I had no time to think; all I could do was react. I had seen my dad with the gun before, and I knew where he kept the clips in the garage. He told me to go grab the clip. I was so scared and confused. He had this ghastly look upon his face, and his eyes were glazed over. It wasn't my dad. I started to cry and refused to get the clip for him. I knew that whatever was going on was bad. I pleaded with him and tried my hardest to defuse the situation. Feeling helpless, I finally relented and went to the garage and grabbed the clip. This action caused me so much remorse and guilt later on in life. I blamed myself for what transpired and for the innocent lives that were drastically impacted by the ripple effect of this incident. If only I hadn't gotten that clip. . . .

I brought him the clip wrapped in a bandana and watched as he unfolded it and grabbed it in his hand. The jarring sound of the clip being pushed into the butt of the gun sent chills through my body. Immediately Uncle Mike appeared and prompted my siblings and me to follow him. There was panic in the air. I knew this feeling; it was the same insidious energy I experienced on the nights my mother overdosed. Fear, uncertainty, confusion. We got into my uncle's car to leave the house and were stopped around the corner by a parade of sheriffs. Uncle Mike had called the cops before we left in fear of what my dad might do with the loaded pistol he was brandishing. The cops were blocking the street with their vehicles, so there was no way out, and we were forced to the side of the road. We were told not to move. Everything was happening quickly. A whirlwind of thoughts flooded my mind as I saw the officers pulling their guns out and positioning themselves around the parked cars. They were preparing for a gunfight. It was dusk and getting darker by the second.

Suddenly I heard the roar of an engine and lights coming toward us from down the street. I saw how tense the sheriffs were becoming as they scrambled into position. We were in a very precarious situation if shots rang out, so they yelled over to us to get down in our car. I saw my dad come racing around the corner in his car as the officers stood, guns drawn and yelling commands in his direction. I couldn't believe what I was seeing; I was in complete shock and awe. As the cops were yelling, I lay down on the floor of the car as my younger brother and sister clung to me. I'll never forget my brother's arms gripping tightly around me as he repeated, "Please, Sean. Please, Sean. I love you, Sean." It was heart-wrenching to hear his pleas for help. The little details we remember from the traumatic experiences in life—his voice ringing in my ears as he cried—perpetuate for eternity.

For a moment, it was as if time slowed down and everything was silent. I know the cops were still yelling at my dad to get out of the car, but I was almost oblivious to it. All I was focused on was anticipating the first gunshot to ring out. It was inevitable. I couldn't believe what was happening and how quickly this situation had escalated. It was all my fault. Why did I give him that clip? Was my dad going to be killed? Were gunshots going to enter our car? What was going to happen? A million thoughts raced through my mind in those fleeting seconds. Any second, the gunshots would come.

Then, before I knew it, it was over. My dad had surrendered, and I sat up to see the officers put him into the back of one of the cop cars, handcuffed. The fact that it ended that way was a miracle. I cannot believe he wasn't shot. That is what I had expected, and the thought of my dad being killed in front of my siblings and me was torturous in itself. I'll never forget lying on the floor of

Uncle Mike's car, squeezed next to my brother and sister, scared and in disbelief as to what we just witnessed.

The ripple effect of this incident would send a string of devastating events into motion that would alter our lives forever. Nothing would ever be the same from that moment on. In what felt like a split second, my life was shattered.

.

THE AFTERMATH & MY LOST YEARS

When my father was arrested, it truly broke my heart. I was demoralized and completely caught off guard. I can't explain the pain and shock that I felt in the days after his arrest. Sadness and emptiness overcame me. Although I was fourteen and a freshman in high school, I was still very naive and innocent, unprepared to cope with the traumatic events I was experiencing. For the first time in my life, I saw the world through a darker lens. I saw and felt pain and hopelessness unlike anything I had known. Up until then, I had been sheltered from that part of life, so when I was exposed to it, it hit me like a paralyzing force of energy I couldn't withstand.

I had no idea that this was only the beginning of our demise as a family; it was a fast-moving chain reaction I was totally unprepared for. My mother unraveled after my father's arrest. My parents had been unhappy for years and had grown increasingly at odds. With my father out of the picture, on his way to prison for several years, my mom saw this as her chance to get away. She didn't waste a minute. It might have been months after my dad's arrest, but it felt like the very next day that she abandoned us. Rather than protect and care for her children, she sought to heal her own wounds and her addiction soon got the best of her. She left us at the most critical time of our young lives. At first, she would just be gone for a day, then it turned to two or three days, and eventually, she was gone for weeks at a time. I couldn't make sense of it. I was still trying to cope with my father being gone.

In the blink of an eye, I lost both my parents. I remember feeling that death would be easier than dealing with the emotions and heartache I felt. The pain was so overwhelming and wreaked havoc on my life. Instead of sleeping, I lay awake, tossing and turning as my insides churned. It felt like the emotional toll was squeezing and suffocating the life out of me. I would go into the bathroom and stare at myself in the mirror, trying to understand what was going on. Tears would stream down my face. I was suffering so much and I felt so alone. I still had Uncle Mike and my brother and sister, but there was a piece inside that was gone. I could no longer feel the love I experienced as a kid, and the passion for life I once had was dying. I could feel a void starting to expand, a void I felt would consume my entire life. It was like a plague, an inexorable blight killing everything in sight.

I had no idea how to put the pieces back together of my shattered life. My Uncle Mike tried to save me. He did everything he could to give me love and guidance. He stepped into the role of mother, father, and provider without hesitation. He saw how devastated we were, and he just wanted to give us love and security for our future. He possessed so much love and showered it upon my siblings and me unconditionally. But it was too late. I was lost and already too far gone to be saved.

In less than a year, everything in my life was fragmented and scattered in a million different directions. My dad was in prison somewhere I didn't want to think about. My mother was nowhere to be found most of the time. And I was aimlessly adrift with no purpose or direction. I don't know what was worse, missing my parents or being reminded of what they had become. I missed the parents I once had in my life. My dad was gone and my mom was a shadow of the person I once knew. It broke my heart to see her that way; she was more like a stranger than the mother I had grown up with.

This was one of the toughest times of my life. All the pain and emotions were fresh and intense. I had no recourse, no way to make things better. All I knew was that I couldn't face what was happening, I couldn't accept what my life was coming to. I refused to accept it. Feeling out of control and hopeless, the only thing I could do was pretend it wasn't real. Deep down inside, I couldn't hide from the truth, but on the surface, I learned to mask the pain and found my own way to escape.

Almost instantly, I had turned to drugs and alcohol to numb the unbearable pain I was facing. It was the only thing I could do to find temporary relief from my devastating thoughts and emotions. Just as our family had fallen apart so quickly, I seemed to change overnight. Everything about me changed. My attitude and demeanor grew careless and indifferent. I became self-conscious and ashamed of who I was, and I lost my spark for life. I didn't love myself. I didn't love my life anymore.

As I began drinking and smoking every day—it was the only thing I found to quiet the tormenting thoughts in my head—I started hanging out with a new group of friends who had similar interests or life experiences as I had. I'm not sure if it was because unconsciously I wanted to be around people I could relate to more because being around my old friends and seeing their families and their pleasant lives was too painful. Looking back, I think I was just so ashamed and didn't want people I had known to see me like that. I was afraid people who knew who I was before could see through my facade to the truth I tried so hard to keep hidden. I couldn't face them because that would force me to acknowledge everything going on. It was easier to avoid certain people and places that triggered my dark thoughts and emotions. I would rather stay numb than face reality.

Subsequently, my mind and my life started to become warped. I stopped going home and avoided anything that reminded me of my old life. Sports, old friends, family members, the beach; I hid from it all. At the age of fifteen, I hardly saw my siblings or Uncle Mike.

Getting high or drunk so I could momentarily forget about all my problems quickly resulted in a dependency and eventually a full-blown addiction to drugs and alcohol. It was a toxic relationship, but I was blind to it all. I thought drugs and alcohol could help me avoid the pain and despair forever. But over time, I just suppressed my emotions rather than resolve them. I didn't understand this at the time, though. I was just trying to survive. However, the more I numbed myself and checked out, the deeper I fell into the abyss.

By sixteen, I was living an entirely different life. I felt like a different person; I was behaving differently and talking differently. The scary part is that I actually started to identify with the person I had created. I smoked cigarettes and marijuana. I drank alcohol. I got into fights. I told myself that was who I was now. My mind was warped and I had less and less connection with the loving kid within I had once been.

I thought I was protecting myself, but I was failing miserably. My attempts to numb the pain and escape reality made everything worse. I was getting in trouble at school and was disconnected from my family, heading down a dark, self-destructive path. People who knew me were confused by my behavior.

Essentially, I was following in the footsteps of my parents whom I had grown to resent. Everything was so distorted—my thinking, my relationships, my life. As if the initial demise and breakdown of our family structure wasn't enough to deal with, my dad came back home for a short time after he got out of prison. The next four to five years were a constant battle that forced me to experience the pain and despair over and over again.

My dad would come and go from jail, and my mom would often show up high on drugs and cause a commotion. This was like a never-ending onslaught of pain and torture. Part of my siblings and I wanted them around because we still clung to hope that one day things could go back to how they once were. But time and time again, we were let down and disappointed. It seemed like nothing would ever get better, and our lives spiraled into complete chaos.

I felt that my mother never really tried to change her ways. She never was able to rebound from her addiction, and by then, she had inflicted permanent damage to herself. She was utterly lost. Every time I saw her in that state, I felt all the heartbreak and devastation resurface. It was unbearable. I developed deep resentment toward her because I couldn't understand why she continued to cause us so much harm. To see my mother completely change into a different person because of her drug use was one of the most sorrowful things I've experienced in my life. Words alone can't describe how hard it was for me to witness firsthand.

My father was different too. Coming home and seeing the aftermath of what he'd caused was too much for him. My mom had left him, my siblings and I were distant and trying to move on in our lives, and he still had his own demons to battle. My dad had also experienced a childhood marked by painful and traumatic events and had turned to drugs and alcohol to numb his pain and quiet the noise, just as I was. It was a vicious cycle that was now being perpetuated in my life. Still, at that time, I had no idea how insidious this affliction truly was and how it could destroy everything. I was so upset and confused by my dad's actions. I felt like he never tried to get back to the way things were, and he instead chose a selfish path that affected everything and everyone around him.

From the time I was sixteen to twenty-one, my home was like a war zone. The cops were there regularly, looking for my dad or responding to a disturbance. My mother would show up intoxicated or completely delusional. I can't even count all the times the cops were called for a fight or argument taking place at our house. It became almost a daily part of life as sad as that is to say. It was complete and utter chaos. The alcohol and drug abuse combined with all the unresolved pain was a recipe for disaster. In the midst of it, I felt that my parents didn't care about anything or anyone else. I was resentful toward them for continuing to cause so much harm and bringing all that pain into our lives. My anger toward them distorted my attitude and perspective tremendously, and I eventually turned my anger on myself.

I thought I could suppress my anger, frustration, shame, and self-loathing by staying high every day. However, at times my emotions would surface uncontrollably. Out of nowhere, I would burst into tears or become enraged and start a fight at school or parties for no reason. I was humiliated by my inability to control myself. Walking around feeling tense and upset became my homeostasis, my permanent state of being.

Holding it all in became unbearable and the pain and unresolved issues would come out emphatically when I was drunk. I would express all the emotions I worked tirelessly to suppress. Then I would wake up the next day feeling ashamed and embarrassed. This was a recurring pattern throughout my adolescence that only reinforced my negative view of the world and myself. Somewhere inside me, I knew this wasn't who I was, but I had no idea how to break the pattern.

My biggest problem was that I refused to face the reality of my situation. At school, teachers and peers wanted to ask me questions and talk to me about my personal life. It was obvious to them how much pain I was in and how much different I'd become. They all wanted to help me and tried to be there for me. Every time I came home, Uncle Mike would try to have a serious talk with me. He cared so much about my well-being and did everything he could to help me, but we became at odds because I wouldn't open up and talk to him.

I couldn't open up to anybody. I wouldn't talk about what had transpired the previous two years because that would mean it was real. What was I going to say? That my parents left us and came back high on drugs and alcohol and made our lives miserable every day? It hurt to think it let alone express it to someone else.

All I ever thought about as a little kid was playing high school sports, going to college, and becoming a professional athlete. I had dreams I was inspired to pursue. There was no fear or doubt about my abilities and what I could accomplish if I put my mind to it. But now, I had given up on any dream or desire I ever had as a kid. I never once talked to a coach or even thought about playing sports in high school. My confidence and self-esteem had been shattered, and I dared not put myself in a position to be seen or noticed. It felt as though the shame and embarrassment I felt deep within could be seen by anyone I made eye contact with. I felt like they could see through my flesh and into my suffocating soul.

Ultimately, I ended up a bystander watching my life pass by. I saw other people who were able to live their lives and be themselves, but I felt stuck, too heartbroken and distraught to follow their good examples.

Despite the life I was choosing to live, I still had brief instances of hope that things could get better one day. In certain moments reality would hit me that I had just watched four years of my life pass me by without living as the person I knew I was capable of being.

And when that happened, I would feel a stirring, but I would dismiss the thought and feeling. But they were there, below the surface.

I didn't realize how vital these instances were at the time, but they served to keep my spirit alive. Though I never fully applied myself in high school, I somehow managed to get my diploma anyway. It was uneventful, and even though I was graduating, I hadn't felt like I earned anything. I remember all the kids acting so excited and optimistic for the future, but I couldn't relate. I wanted so badly to share in their excitement—to talk about college and our future aspirations, to feel excited, and to envision an auspicious future full of possibilities. But I couldn't see it. I couldn't feel that energy, nor could I believe in it ever coming true.

I remember the summer afterward, I showed up at the beach where all the kids I grew up playing sports with were playing tackle football. I hadn't socialized with them much in the past four years, but we still got along and they would say hi in the hallways at school. They asked me to play with them, and I remember feeling so good running up and down the beach. In those particular moments, I felt like a kid again. There were no concerns or fears overwhelming me. I let my wall down and let myself just be in the moment.

I'll never forget that day. Some girls and other friends were watching us. I wasn't the biggest guy out there, but I still knew how to play. I always had. People used to tell me I was a natural when it came to sports, and I always felt in my element playing pretty much anything. I'll never forget one specific play on that day. The biggest kid out there, probably close to 300 pounds, had the ball and was running straight for me. It was like slow motion. I didn't budge and remember hitting him with my shoulder right at the waist and him flying backward. I was shocked at how he went down, and everyone started yelling and cheering. That was one of the only times in high school I did something in front of my peers that got recognition. Not because I was incapable but because I was holding back. I missed out on everything I could have been or done because of my pain and how tormented I was. I was allowing those unresolved memories and emotions to control me and ruin my life. I was ashamed for being so weak and not living as the person I wanted to be, but I just felt unable to break free. However, that day in that one brief moment, I proved to myself that I still had it.

There were some brief moments like that throughout my adolescence when I felt connected to my old self, my true self! They proved to me that that side of me was still alive. But the sad thing is, that was enough for me. Rather than take that as a sign or use that momentum to break out of my rut and start living life the way I truly wanted to, I just accepted that as enough. Something internal was still holding me back from permanently stepping into the version of myself I knew I could be.

When I had fleeting moments where I had a desire to live my life differently and stop allowing all that precious time to pass me by, I was often intoxicated and under the influence of some substance. Suddenly my wall would be lowered and emotions and feelings I worked so hard to suppress would surface. This wasn't always the bad emotions I described earlier either. Sometimes I'd talk about doing good in my life and making something of myself. That day at the beach, I talked with everyone about going to city college and playing football. Everyone told me how great I'd be, and I had no doubt that I could do it. We were drinking and it all seemed so easy.

But once the effects of the alcohol wore off the next day, I dismissed any notion of taking action to change my life and pursue my passions. It was like two polar energies were alive inside me: the kid who wanted to live and experience life and the scared and broken teenager not ready to let go. I felt more connected to the negative image of who I'd become because that was the person I was breathing life into through my daily thoughts and actions. However, moments like that one at the beach kept my spirit alive within. I didn't know it at the time, but below all the shame and self-loathing, there was still the kid full of love and life. He hadn't given up.

After graduating high school, I had no plan or vision of what I wanted to do with my life. Since I had just been in survival mode, the previous four years were a blur, so I had nothing to draw upon for inspiration going into adulthood. I never thought about what I truly wanted for myself, but I knew I wanted more than the life I was living. That sentiment was always with me, below the surface like a faint whisper I couldn't completely ignore, but I was numb, too numb to feel this desire most of the time. I was devoid of that creative energy where dreams derive and the swelling tide of passion can compel us to act.

Time was passing, and as I approached adulthood, I knew I wouldn't be able to hide behind my age or the wrongdoings of my parents. The relentless feeling of "I can't continue to live like this" started to emerge. But with I had no foundation, nothing to grow on, I was still lost. I felt stuck. The only thing I really identified with was my addiction to drugs and alcohol and the toxic relationships that came with it.

Two of the most powerful forces in our external environment are the relationships we have and the company we keep. At this time in my life, I attracted people and situations that coincided with my internal belief system and my own self-image. After graduating high school, I continued to surround myself with people I felt comfortable with, who I could relate to. In retrospect, this was one of my biggest mistakes. I was never challenged by my peers, never inspired to go above and beyond. We only reinforced our pain and internal struggles through the daily actions and lifestyle we chose. My future was bleak.

I had little to no self-confidence because I hadn't done anything with my life. It was a perpetuating cycle. Feeling bad about not living the life I desired crushed my self-esteem. The doubt and insecurity I experienced as a result would justify not doing anything to break this pattern. I was reinforcing my self-defeating thoughts and behaviors, everything I wanted to change, by not doing anything about it. The longer this went on, the bigger the gap grew between my current life and the life I aspired to live. I surrounded myself with people who would not remind me of that, so it was easy to stay stuck and give less to life as I did. But it ate away at me. Most of the time, this was occurring unconsciously. I knew I could do more with my life. I knew I was capable of more. I just couldn't take that first scary step. All the pressure, all the weight I was carrying around was getting heavier. I was stuck and any escape from that predicament felt out of my grasp.

Had it not been for an opportunity to work for one of my uncles doing hard, physical labor, I would have hit rock bottom much more quickly.

This was the opportunity I needed. It may not have appeared very significant on the surface, but it had a huge impact on me. The experience instilled confidence and belief in myself that had been lost and forgotten. Seeing the results of my effort day in, day out helped me start to construct a much healthier self-image. I had something in my life to look forward to, something I took pride in. Every day I would get up early and mentally prepare myself for a long day of hard work. I was able to channel the energy I had been suppressing all those years into my work ethic. I took pride in what I was doing, held the belief that I could excel at a task when I put my mind to it, and gained the confidence that comes when you apply yourself and succeed. I was able to start tapping back into the energy and mentality I thought I had lost, the same energy I experienced when I was out on the baseball diamond or surfing with my friends. It was that same spark I felt the day I played football on the beach—the energy of life and passion and my untapped potential that had been waiting for an opportunity to shine all those years. I could feel it calling to be unleashed.

I started to breathe life into a better version of myself through my actions and effort. It was subtle at first, but I was living more like the person I knew I could become and less like the afflicted individual I had been.

I prided myself on working hard and quickly realized how, when I applied myself, I could do things well. The lessons I was able to take away from these years of hard work were carried onward with me for the rest of my life. I was able to forge a mindset composed of discipline, self-confidence, pride, and ownership in what I was doing. Soon, the changes I was making started to impact my loved ones as well.

At this time Uncle Mike was out of work due to an injury, and I was able to help in a way I never had before. It felt good to contribute at home financially. My Uncle Mike had always worked hard to provide for my siblings and me, working long hours with almost no days off for years. He did whatever it took to keep a roof over our head and food on the table. We didn't have a lot, but Uncle Mike made sure we had everything we needed.

Since Uncle Mike couldn't work, he agreed to let my dad move back in. We needed the income to keep the house and survive. When he moved back in, our relationship took on a different form than it ever had before.

My father and I spent nearly every moment together. He was experienced in the work I was learning, and it was helpful to have him around when I started. We would work hard, side by side all day, and then head home together. This felt great in the moment. I was finally close to him, and we were sharing time together we never had before. This is what I had longed for my entire life. I hoped he would finally make a change to get sober and be the father I wanted so badly. My whole life I had just wanted him to be sober. But every time he did, there was a brief moment of hope, inevitably followed by a dramatic letdown. Getting drunk and arrested, kicked out of his sober living house, being homeless, going back to prison; it was a never-ending cycle I experienced throughout my high school years. For years I had been let down, but somehow each time he vowed to get sober, I thought it was actually a possibility. Being so close with my dad and wanting so badly for him to change set me up for letdown after letdown, and each time, I was devastated.

There were some positives. My father is a good man with a big heart. He offered moral support and helped me feel good about myself for the work I was doing. He helped me to find a confidence I had been lacking most of my life, and I felt extremely grateful for the influence he had on me in this regard. I could always see the good in him, even when others didn't. I believed in him and wanted nothing more than to see him happy and healthy. However, he had internal issues that he could never resolve. His entire life he had been avoiding his pain and numbing himself. He did the best he could, at least that's what I want to believe. But his pain was unbearable and he could never make the permanent changes he wanted.

It escalated to the point where my dad would get completely wasted at the job site and get kicked off, or he would blackout at home. When he wasn't passed out, he'd often start a confrontation for no apparent reason. It was torture, honestly. Every day, everyone was on edge and no one knew what was to come. The worst part of all was that I felt caught in the middle. Here I was feeling so good about having this bond and relationship with my dad that I had wanted my entire life. But my dependency on drugs and alcohol was growing worse every day. I couldn't see that I was becoming more and more like my dad.

No matter what happened, I was always there by his side, and I didn't realize how much I was being affected.

In the moment, I thought it was great to share a beer after work and listen to him tell stories about his own upbringing. We finally had a common bond in the fact that we were working at the same place and both helping support the family. We both felt good about it. I never thought twice about handing over the money I made, week after week. It was an honor and the greatest accomplishment of my life up to that point. I remember my friends asking why I gave all my money away, but I didn't see it like that at all. Family was everything to me, and I would do anything to help out and support my loved ones. This was one of the values I never lost sight of even through my darkest times. In my eyes family was everything. Ironically, this deeply rooted belief and my unyielding loyalty to my father became more harmful over time as our relationship grew increasingly toxic.

To complicate matters, I hadn't dealt with all the anger I had suppressed about how he behaved after his arrest. I felt like he had given up. Yeah, I was happy to rekindle our relationship, but I still had so much unresolved pain within.

What began to manifest was a distorted and volatile relationship fueled by alcohol and codependency.

The worst part was that it took a toll on my relationship with Uncle Mike. He would get upset with my dad and threaten to kick him out, and I would find myself trying to mediate between the two. I was constantly preventing a full-blown fight or trying to calm my dad down when he was enraged. He was like a tyrant, but I couldn't turn my back on him. I just couldn't. But I felt a lot of guilt and shame for siding with him because I knew his actions were devastating my family.

I was relentlessly confronted by so many issues both internally and externally. Unresolved anger and addiction, my false bravado and lack of true self-identity, my dad's confrontational behavior, trying to mediate between him and Uncle Mike or him and my siblings or him and the cops. It was exhausting. Despite the chaos, I was still drinking with my dad and very much contributing to our unhealthy relationship. I wasn't a victim here—at least that's not the picture I wanted to paint.

One day, I was with a friend out front of our home and my little brother, who must have been eight years old, came running out yelling, "Dad OD'd! Dad OD'd!" I immediately ran inside to find my father unconscious on the bathroom floor, his lifeless body keeled over. I picked him up and carried him into the bedroom without hesitation. Immediately, I started to perform CPR as Uncle Mike called the paramedics. I don't know how long this lasted; I just knew I wasn't going to let my father die on the floor in front of everyone. Time became irrelevant. I couldn't hear or think of anything aside from each breath I gave to my dad's lifeless body. Nothing was happening, no matter how much oxygen I was breathing into him, he wouldn't wake or budge. Just one sign, one noise or movement was all I needed to hear. All my senses were enhanced in anticipation of that split second to know that he was alive. Finally, I heard a gurgling noise come from the depths of my father. In that moment, I felt a surge of hope. I knew then that he was going to survive.

The paramedics finally came in and took him off on a stretcher. I went to my room and sat down on the bed, staring off in disbelief, feeling numb and in shock. I'll never forget that moment sitting there all alone. It was dreamlike; I was observing myself and my life from what felt like a different vantage point. As if I was looking down upon our lives, I was just a bystander in that moment— free of pain or distress. What had my life come to? Why was this happening? Why did it all change so drastically for us? I was almost in a trance, a meditative state looking back on all the painful memories and incidents over the years. My dad's arrest, my mother leaving, the shame and despair I felt, the drug and alcohol abuse, lost dreams, anger, resentments, pain, remorse. It flooded my consciousness and was coursing through me in a flash of images. I could never escape or erase those images. I was as close as possible to giving up at that moment. Part of me felt like I already had. I was contributing to these events indirectly. Was I a culprit or a victim? I was so confused. But I did have one very powerful realization and that was how resilient I had become. As harsh as these life lessons were, they were hardening me for the arduous journey ahead. I didn't know why at the time, but something within kept fighting and helped me get back up every time I was knocked down.

My father survived that overdose and we all acted as if nothing happened. We were quick to move on and avoid talking about the severity of our predicament and how fragile life had become. As was our m.o., it was easier to avoid it altogether. The pain, the shame, the distorted lives we led. It had become normal, but anytime I left to go out with friends, I had a nervous feeling in the pit of my stomach. It was the same feeling I had as a kid: impending doom. The same feeling I got when I saw that ambulance heading toward our home after my mom overdosed; the feeling I would get whenever the grown-ups were talking loud and arguing; the same feeling I had in my recurring nightmare. This was the feeling I had been running from my entire life. The joy and love that had once connected us were fading fast.

By the time I was twenty-one, my addiction had intensified. I spent my time high and intoxicated. Not a day passed without me taking a handful of pills, smoking marijuana, drinking alcohol, or doing it all. I was in bad shape. I was good at hiding it, though. No one knew the extent of my pain or my addiction. I had learned how to mirror what others needed to see in me, never letting on that I was heading down the same path my parents were on, the same insidious death march.

I was still working at this point, but I have no idea how I was able to hold it together with all the partying and substance abuse. I would stay up until one or two in the morning, and then get up for work a couple of hours later. Often, I would wake up still intoxicated from the night before. I would smoke a joint before work, and there were times I was climbing a hundred feet up in the air using a chainsaw in that condition. I would pride myself on the ability to stay up partying all night then outwork everyone the next day. I thought I was invincible. It's stunning to think my false bravado could have easily killed me. It's a miracle, an undeniable act of divine intervention, that I didn't die in an accident at work or in my sleep after a night of drug abuse. I never would have ended my life in those days through an intentional act, but looking back, it's clear I was making an unconscious attempt. I still can't believe I didn't die. So many others who were close to me in those days didn't make it out alive. God had a purpose for me I couldn't see. As desperate as I was, a part of me could always feel it. I just didn't know how to harness that energy yet.

My greatest attempts to change were futile. I was too weak and dependent on external remedies for my condition. Always looking outward, I dared not look within, nor did I understand the extent of my problems and how to overcome them.

I tried to save myself by moving out of my hometown and staying with a family member an hour away. Uncle Mike and my siblings stayed while my girlfriend and I moved away. For a moment, life slowed down and felt better than it had in years. I was away from my parents, old friends, the destructive environment, and the chaos we all had experienced in San Como Way. Despite these changes, I was still very much the same wounded and confused person. I still wasn't living or acting as my true self. There were brief moments of progress, but nothing that lasted. I was incarcerated long before I ever found myself inside a prison. I was a prisoner of my own making.

At that realization, I knew I wanted something more for myself, though. Something inside of me told me I had to get sober. My addiction had caused so much unnecessary turmoil over the years, and I was ready to admit that and make a change.

First I quit smoking, then I focused on quitting alcohol. I was so tired of feeling like a prisoner to my addiction. My attempts to numb myself had just made everything worse.

I thought I could just move on, as if it was that simple. However, with the amount of emotional trauma I had suppressed over the years, moving on would not be that easy. It would be nearly impossible without addressing, and to an extent, reliving, everything from the past I had run away from.

I never thought much about it in those days, at least not in-depth. Any time old memories or feelings would come up, I would get angry or ignore the emotions. Even when I did accumulate several forced months of sobriety, I was still irritable and unhappy. They call this a dry drunk, still having the same behaviors and characteristics of the addict because you're a person still afflicted by their underlying problems.

This started to take a toll on my relationship, and despite the fact that we were living together, I grew estranged from my girlfriend. Luckily, I learned so much during that time, mainly through my own mistakes and inexperience with relationships. This, like many of the difficult lessons I learned in my lifetime, would turn out to be a blessing in disguise. If I had been able to understand that then, I would have saved myself some heartache. But that's not how it works. The pain and the struggle are where wisdom and growth derive. Without the emotional impact, the lesson would not be as great. The mystery of the universe is unpredictable and the lessons we learn can feel and appear cruel in the moment. But everything I endured in my life has helped me to grow, and I have learned more from the bad times than I ever have from the good ones. What was the universe trying to tell me? It was as if I was stuck in a cyclical pattern, and every go-around, I sank lower into the abyss. How could I break free and end this once and for all?

By then, both my parents were homeless. I would go visit them every so often to make sure they were alive. I missed them and loved them despite the heartache they had caused. It was devastating to witness them in such a precarious condition. Every time I saw them, it only reinforced all the pain I had worked so hard to move on from. Seeing my mom looking disheveled and intoxicated felt like a knife stabbing through my heart all over again. What could I do!? It killed me inside.

One day as I made my way down to the beach where my dad stayed, I found him lying in the sand, nearly unrecognizable. He hadn't shaved and was about thirty pounds underweight. He was drunk and extremely malnourished. He looked grim and he could barely talk. It looked like he was close to death. I carried him to my car and decided to bring him back to my one-bedroom cottage. You can imagine how this appeared to my girlfriend at the time. We only had one bedroom and no space to take anyone else in. I didn't care, I couldn't stand the thought of allowing my dad to die on the beach. I was still afflicted by our codependent relationship to the point that I would sacrifice anything to help him out, including my relationship, my sobriety, and my own well-being. I loved my dad tremendously, after all, he is my father. I didn't think twice about my decision, and I couldn't see the harm this would cause.

What was initially only going to be a week turned into two, then a month, and eventually six months. At first, my dad was grateful to have a place to stay and things went smoothly. He has this amazing ability to recover and look as healthy and sprightly as ever in a very short time. I'm still amazed at all he put his body through over the years with his alcohol and drug abuse. He even started to work again with me for my uncle's tree service. However, that was short-lived and things quickly fell apart. Eventually, the same behaviors and scenarios from our old home played out. My dad started drinking daily and it felt like we were back on the front lines. This was the beginning of the end. It was like reliving the previous years all over again.

My girlfriend finally left. We had been unhappy for some time, and I sabotaged our relationship through my careless actions: bringing my dad home to live with us, neglecting the relationship, and focusing only on myself.

Yes, I was the reason she left. And I was the reason I was in so much pain. I had brought it upon myself, thinking for some reason that I could save him. It was that same persistent feeling of hopefulness that got continuously crushed. Every time I got my hopes up, I was setting myself up for failure. It was like reliving the first time he was arrested, or when he overdosed, or all the days after work he terrorized our household. The distress of those incidents was still very alive within me. How naive could I be? Why did I continue to bring this harm upon myself?

Was I just as much to blame as my dad or the drugs and alcohol?

The complexity of our relationship was just as perplexing and harmful to me as my own alcohol and drug addiction. All of these suppressed feelings and emotions intertwined with my maladaptive coping and dysfunctional relationships were like a storm brewing inside of me. How was I still surviving? How had I not imploded or gone crazy?

Then, I did implode. I was so ashamed because I finally gave it a shot to start living my own life and break the cycle. I had moved away from the painful memories of my childhood, was in a committed relationship, had a nice place of my own, and even a career—but I had thrown it all away. I lost sight of the future I wanted to create. In my mind, that had been my only chance and I couldn't see any future hope.

At this time in my life, I felt like a prisoner trapped inside a mind and a life I didn't want.

I didn't want to be dependent on drugs and alcohol, I didn't want to worry about my parents, I didn't want to be in a relationship, I didn't want this life anymore.

Despairingly, I soaked up every ounce of pain and remorse to the fullest. I could never forget how that felt. It was the first time I had gone through a breakup with anyone that I had shared my life with. In the moment, my heartache pierced deep.

I was aware that I had chosen my dad over the relationship; however, I was unprepared for how it impacted me. Suddenly I felt alone and out of place. Despite my dad being there with me and working full-time, I felt off. I recall being overwhelmed by how hard it all hit me and wondered if I had made a mistake. I had let things fall apart and I blamed myself entirely.

Any hope that was forged when I moved away, any thought that life could somehow be different—be better or maybe normal—it was all crushed. I quickly reverted to the same mentality that I had created at fourteen; I reacted the way I always had. I was the same kid attempting to protect myself from my dad's arrest and my mother's abandonment.

However, for all that was the same, there was still something different now. It wasn't like the other painful moments I had endured. I felt a darker and more sinister foreboding. All my sorrows, the unresolved wounds of my past, and my current melancholy were converging. All the emotions were compounded. I was a mess, and I turned to alcohol and drugs heavily. I gave way entirely to my addiction and didn't hold back. It was almost as if I had a death wish; the amount of alcohol and pills I put into my body daily was insane. I just wanted to be numb. I didn't want to feel.

My life had been one painful moment after the next for the past decade. I had been fighting for so long; it's all I knew. The grit and will to survive was deeply ingrained in me. But I couldn't take it any longer. I felt the energy draining from me, leaving me unable to shield myself from the agony and despair I felt within.

I was in so much pain all those years; I can't adequately describe how tormented I truly felt. When I was a kid I couldn't process what was happening fully, but this time I could, and all the realizations of my failures came crashing down upon me. Failure in high school, failure to play sports, failure to be me, failure in my relationship, failure to save my parents. And all of these failures were killing me inside. When we start to live in a depressed state and wallow in our misery, that can be a dangerous place. I imagine this is where suicide, overdose, and other nefarious actions stem from. I was so close and I was feeding that negativity in my thoughts and actions.

Despite my actions, I did want out of that life. But I thought these feelings were going unnoticed by the universe and that I was the only one aware of my emotions. Little did I know that all my wishes would be granted. That I would have the opportunity to face my fears and correct my faults. Oftentimes in life, we get exactly what we need. It's just not always in the fashion we had hoped for.

This time was one of the most impactful learning lessons of my life. I couldn't see it then, but this experience was a blessing in disguise. How could I ever fathom that I would look back on all my struggles with gratitude one day? As if they were made FOR me, to help me and not hurt me as I thought. That all my pain, every heartache, every mistake, every suppressed emotion, every wrong decision, every wasted opportunity, every excuse, every regret, every ounce of negativity, and all the battles I had been incessantly fighting since fourteen would start to make sense. I had to endure these moments; my life depended on it.

THE NIGHT
ON THE MESA

I've never experienced anything in my life like I did the night on the Mesa. It wasn't just the severity of what transpired that was unique, but also the feeling I had within. I've looked back on the night in vivid imagery, going over the details and events as they unfolded. Looking back, it feels the same as it did at the time—felt like an out-of-body experience; it was as if I was acting out scenes instead of living them. Or even more bizarre, I didn't even feel like I was in the first person. I was observing and looking on from a third-party perspective. I have felt that ever since that night, and at the time, I couldn't understand why.

Earlier that day, I was at home waiting for my friend (I will refer to him as Joey for clarity in describing this situation) to pick me up so we could head to Santa Barbara. I wasn't working that day, so I started drinking and taking pills early. It's unfathomable to think of how much poison I put into my body on a daily basis back then. This day, in particular, it was as if I had a death wish, though.

Joey picked me up sometime in the afternoon, and we headed out. I don't recall what we did, but I assume it involved drinking. At some point, we heard about a party in an area of Santa Barbara called "the Mesa." Because I didn't know the people throwing the party, I almost didn't go. I actually made other plans to go out to downtown Santa Barbara and meet some other people. But we decided to stop at the Mesa briefly, then make our way downtown.

When we arrived, I didn't see anyone I recognized so Joey and I started to socialize with the other partiers. Then I saw an old friend, Jasmine, and I started talking with her and a group of friends she was with. We all hung out and talked for a while. I knew Jasmine's friends through mutual acquaintances, but I had never talked with them prior to this night. Up until then, it had been a typical house party with people drinking and carrying on conversations. Suddenly an argument broke out in the kitchen, grabbing the attention of everyone at the party. It isn't uncommon for fights to erupt at parties, so I thought this was just a typical altercation. The argument had been between Jasmine's friends and some guys I had never seen before. However, the fight died down, and we all went back to what we were doing. I heard that the argument was about some old dispute that was apparently never resolved. Several times we got ready to leave the party, but for whatever reason, we kept putting it off. Finally, Joey and I decided to head out and we made our way to the front door.

When we stepped outside to leave, we saw the two groups of guys arguing again. Suddenly everyone was face to face on the front lawn, and it was apparent a fight was looming. I was observing it all, prepared for an altercation. I had been in this very same predicament countless times growing up. Toward the end of the night when the booze took hold and our inhibitions dropped, there was always an altercation. But this night, the one that has since transformed my life forever, was different from all the others.

Face to face in opposition, suddenly someone was hit. It felt like an all-out war was unleashed as people scattered, wrestled, and fought everywhere. It was a chaotic free-for-all. After the initial strike landed, I took a couple steps back in an attempt to observe the situation. Another guy was staring across from me, and we locked eyes. As we approached each other, suddenly, I was assaulted from the side. I remember bear hugging whoever was crashing into me, and we were getting pushed back fast until I was slammed into a parked car.

We crashed to the ground, and I was on my back, still holding onto this person tightly. I didn't want to let go because I knew I would be struck as soon as my face was visible. All I remember thinking was that I was getting jumped. That some of the guys from the fight had zeroed in on me, and I was expecting to start getting kicked and punched in the head. I had been in situations like this before where a fight at a party turns into one person getting assaulted by several others. It wasn't uncommon. I expected it any second. But nothing happened.

I tried several times to roll the person on top of me over, but he was heavy and I couldn't get out from under him. Finally, with another attempt, I was able to roll him over and immediately punched him twice on the side of the head. It was instinct. At this point, it felt like survival and the smartest thing I could do to ensure I wasn't hit in the face as we both jockeyed for positioning. My punches grazed the side of his head, never really connecting flush. So I was surprised when I rose to my feet, and he didn't get up after me.

I guessed one of my punches had connected and he was dazed or knocked out. That's all I could think of in that split second as I got to my feet. Suddenly I heard a voice yelling my name, and I turned to the street to see Joey yelling and gesturing for me to come his way. I went to take a step and excruciating pain shot down my leg. I could hardly walk and my left leg didn't want to move. The crash into the parked car had pinched something in my low back. It felt like slow motion as I made my way to my friend, standing only ten feet away in the street. It felt like eternity, like one of those dreams when you want to go faster but your body isn't working properly.

I'll never forget what happened next. As I got to the curb and stepped into the street, the light above illuminated me. I was in shock and horrified to see myself covered in blood. I had never seen that much blood before, and it was dripping off me as if someone had poured a bucket of it over my head. My eyes were covered in blood. I could see it dripping off my face and all over my long-sleeved button-up shirt. My friend looked at me in horror. I think he said something like, "What the hell, Sean? You're covered in blood." It must have been a grim sight.

Next thing I knew, Joey was about five feet ahead of me yelling, "Let's go, let's go!" I started limping up the street but could hardly manage. He disappeared up around the corner and eventually ran back down to show me the way. I was disoriented and acting on impulse. He motioned me to an open door off the street, and I barely made it in as cop cars with their lights on raced by on the street. We were in a laundry room. Amidst the sound of sirens blaring, my friend opened the washer and dryer and found an old shirt. I peeled off my blood-soaked button up and put the other shirt on. Joey told me he had called a cab to pick us up. Sure enough, there was the cab awaiting us down the block. We got in and headed back to his place.

The next twenty-four hours were a blur of confusion, denial, and disbelief. I was disoriented when we got back to my friend's house, and the pain in my low back was so bad, I could hardly move. After my friend helped me out of my blood-soaked clothes, I passed out on his floor. The feeling I had inside me when I woke up the next morning was like when you have a nightmare. But it wasn't a dream. I knew something bad had happened, and I tried to make sense of it all in my head. I just couldn't put all the pieces together. I remember googling "fight on the Mesa" and was shocked to find out two people had been stabbed. I had already come to the conclusion the guy I was wrestling around with must have been stabbed given the amount of blood on me. I didn't know when he was stabbed; I didn't see it, so I couldn't say for sure. But I had no idea another person was stabbed as well. I was confused and in shock. I was numb from the drugs and alcohol. Once I read what had happened, I immediately took another handful of pills and drank more alcohol. Maybe if I numbed myself enough this whole thing would go away. That was the only solution I could think of. After all, that's what I had done my entire life to avoid facing tough times.

Joey was distraught. He knew something serious had happened and someone had gotten hurt. I'm not sure if he really thought I did it or if he was just scared of the repercussions that would soon come. In my head, I assumed he knew I didn't stab anyone. After all, he was right there when I stood up. He would have seen a weapon in my hand if I'd had one. All the while I assumed we were on the same page with everything. If anything, he would be able to clear my name when I was questioned about my actions of punching a guy who had been stabbed at a party. I believed everything would be OK. The truth would come out and my name would be cleared. I was guilty of fighting and leaving the scene, but not of a stabbing. I took my friend's quiet demeanor as a sign that we were on the same page, that when it came time to be confronted about the incident, the truth would set us free. I was completely wrong.

I want to acknowledge something very important here. In my own delusional state, being essentially in survival mode, I was unable to grasp the severity of my situation. I was numbed by drugs and alcohol and in complete denial. One of the men who was assaulted was fighting for his life in the hospital. Later on, reports would surface that he came as close to death as possible without succumbing. Unverified reports stated he died three times that night on the way to the emergency room, and it was a miracle he'd survived. I need to stop here and reflect for a moment. I've been so focused on telling my own story and how this event impacted me that I haven't spoken of this. It is a miracle that man lived. In the midst of it all, I couldn't even connect or empathize with that sentiment, that reality. I couldn't grasp or fully understand the severity of what had transpired.

I lay in bed all the next day, hiding from the world, hoping the situation would all just go away. Or that maybe it was a dream and soon I would awake, out of breath but relieved. How could this have happened!? I knew how bad it must have looked, but I still had a feeble hope that things would be OK. I was foolish and naive. Deep down in my heart, I knew I hadn't done anything malicious. I knew my actions that night had been wrong, that I shouldn't have gotten involved in that fight. But I had no idea the wrath, the awakening that was in store for me.

MY ARREST:
COUNTY JAIL

When the distractions are taken from our lives and we have time to honestly reflect, to peer deep within, it's amazing what we can discover about ourselves. We think we know who we truly are; we get so good at fooling ourselves and allowing the distorted perceptions we create to control the way we live our lives. However, it is not always so.

The next day, I finally attempted to get out and called a friend to pick me up. Joey had since left. I had no idea he was already at the police station. As I drove off, I saw a parade of sheriffs and SWAT officers approaching me. My heart dropped. They pulled us over and ordered us out of the car. I wasn't surprised, I'd suspected something like this was coming. Everything felt like it was in slow motion again. Dogs barking, someone yelling orders at me. As I glanced over my shoulder, I saw six AR-15s pointed right at my face. I was numb. I was scared. I felt disconnected from my body, like I was an onlooker to a devastating situation rather than a key player. Two men had been seriously injured, one had nearly lost his life. Others were being detained and questioned about their actions and involvement.

Upon my arrest and shortly after, I was shaken to the very core of my existence. Everything I had learned, believed in, and understood was challenged in the ensuing months. And I would experience an internal transformation unlike anything I ever could have fathomed. Little did I know, this situation would turn out to be the defining moment of my life.

The first couple nights in the county jail I was miserable. It was dark and cold. I'll never forget the lifeless expression on the other inmates' faces as I walked down the long hallway to my cell. The foul smell of urine and body odor filled the air. As I entered my cell the sound of the door clasping shut sent chills down my spine. Now I was alone and there was nothing I could do to escape my situation. Coming off all the drugs and alcohol put my mind and body through agony. All the poison was being purged from my body. I was still in disbelief that I was in jail, for attempted murder at that. I'll never forget how the detectives acted the night I was arrested. It was like a scene in a movie, with them coming into the room I was confined in and slamming down pictures of the victim. I couldn't believe it was real, not even when they dressed me in the white jumpsuit and drove me to the county jail.

Four others were brought in for questioning about the infamous night on the Mesa. However, I remained the one charged with the heinous crime of attempted murder. I was still in shock on my first day at court, still numb and failing to realize I was not dreaming. I'll never forget the words my lawyer spoke to me that day, "They will most likely adjust your charges to homicide; the victim is brain dead." Can you imagine what I felt in that moment? While I attempted to grasp what my lawyer had just said, members of the Newspress frantically positioned themselves in the courtroom to take my photo. I couldn't even react, I didn't know what to say or feel at this point. I was still in denial. I was numb. Maybe because I knew I was innocent I thought somehow, someway, it would all work out. Despite trying to convince myself of that, it *was* happening and there was nothing I could do. Something far greater was at work within my life.

I awaited my fate for nearly a year, confined in the county jail. I would go back and forth from jail to the courthouse once or twice a month but the majority of my time was spent in a cell. A cell so small I could touch both walls simultaneously. Other than my cellmate, I was in complete isolation from the outside world. We had yard for one hour each day, but the other twenty-three were spent in lockdown. I received visits for one hour on the weekends from family members, and we would correspond through letters and postcards as well. Aside from that, I had no outside contact.

Never in my life had my external circumstances and surroundings been so bleak. I had never been more isolated from the outside world. I felt alone and completely powerless against these forces imposing upon my life. I felt broken and desperate for some form of help or guidance—but there was nothing. I couldn't see or recognize anything that could save me.

Miraculously, the victim in my case survived. After the first court appearance, there was never any talk of amending my charges to homicide, but I knew this was going to be a fight for my life, as I was still charged with attempted murder and faced a maximum penalty of life in prison. All the witnesses from the party who had been questioned made statements saying they saw me on top of the victim striking down at him. The police report painted a horrible picture of me as the assailant. Even my lawyer appeared indifferent and I got the impression everyone felt I was guilty from the beginning. The writing was on the wall and everywhere I went I got the same look and despairing expression. When you come in with a blue band on your wrist, which means you're fighting a life sentence, everyone knows it's serious. I saw how people looked at me when I entered the courtroom or a housing unit at the jail, and I could feel the energy shift immediately. I had no idea what I was in for or how I was going to get through it.

With nothing but an abundance of time and my own thoughts, the biggest challenge I faced was how to stay sane and not allow all the uncertainty to overwhelm me.

Worst-case possibilities and made-up scenarios would destroy me. It was nearly impossible not to dwell or speculate about what was going to happen. How much time in prison would I get? What would my life be like? Would I see my family again? Such a predicament could torture a man to death. However, I knew I couldn't survive if I let my mind entertain those thoughts. Surely I would break.

Living in a cell was so bizarre. All day long, I would look for ways to keep busy and pass the time, to keep me from thinking those disastrous thoughts. It worked for the most part, but when night came and the lights were dimmed, time felt like it slowed down. Suddenly I was alone again. With the distractions of my daily routine gone, my mind would race before I fell asleep. My anxiety became relentless and piercing. I had avoided facing my pain and heartache for a long time, but lying there with no distractions, I couldn't run away or numb myself as I always had.

My freedom, my fate, and my entire life were in jeopardy, but I was transfixed more by my own revelations. I'd never had such an opportunity to think and reflect on my life. As my perspective continued to shift and adjust, I started to realize just how much life I had neglected over the years. How much precious time I had watched pass me by. I experienced despair, frustration, guilt, remorse, and so many painful emotions those first couple months. I couldn't deny or suppress them.

I felt such deep regret that it pierced through my heart and paralyzed me; it was devastating. I couldn't believe this is what it had come to. I thought I had more time— that somehow, miraculously, I was going to get back on track in my life. But that hadn't happened. I couldn't stop thinking about the years I'd wasted. I couldn't stop myself from feeling guilty and ashamed for the path I had chosen. All my mistakes were magnified. Every wrong decision and careless act played over and over in my head.

Since the drugs were out of my system, I could feel everything so intensely. It was painful and disheartening. However, it was completely necessary. In those moments, I felt as close to death as I ever had, as hopeless as I could ever imagine being. Only, this was worse than death because I was still here reliving all the wasted and neglected aspects of my life that I would never get back. I had to live in that pain. I had to embrace it. That was my truth and my reality that I couldn't ignore. Imprisoned with no salvation in sight, it felt like my entire life was over before it had even begun.

I knew I wasn't guilty of the crime they arrested me for, and I experienced a disconnect from that notion altogether. Nevertheless, I did experience a tremendous amount of guilt and remorse for living a life untrue to who I was. That's where I started to focus all my energy. I had so much work to do. I didn't even know who I was at that point, and there was so much to uncover and explore internally.

That's when my real journey began; it was a spiritual journey that took place deep below the surface. For in that cell, that cement box, in those sobering moments when I lay awake before bed, I started to uncover the truth. My truth. The truth I had been hiding from my entire life.

For the first time ever, I was forced to face it, and I had to find a way to create optimism in my life that allowed me to feel good despite my conditions.

So at that point, I started to become more transfixed through self-analysis than anything else. I spent every waking moment analyzing myself, dissecting my life and every intricate detail up till that point. It was like living under a microscope, and I had put myself there out of intuition. I experienced a profound shift in my perception and internal state that changed my life forever. It felt as if the outside world had become increasingly irrelevant. My external circumstances merely served as a reminder of the decisions I had made and the life I had chosen.

It was survival, it was preservation of my mind and my sanity. The ability to create positive energy or find the good in worst-case scenarios massively shifted my psychology. Indirectly, it very well saved my life. I knew this was by far the greatest test I would ever face—not just during my incarceration and my environment.

When life takes on such a solemn undertone—when someone dies, relationships fall apart, or a situation similar to mine transpire—it becomes very clear what does and does not matter. If only we could see it and live by this understanding without having to go through such experiences.

The severity of my situation allowed me to see things in a completely different light. My incarceration; being deprived of amenities, lack of human connection and relationships I had taken for granted; and an abundance of time to think and reflect—these were all blessings in disguise. When they all converged simultaneously, the energy they created was indescribable.

These are the unforgettable moments in life when you find out who you really are and what you're made of. When you cannot escape and you must face your fears, your weaknesses, and your demons head-on.

During this time, a particular memory from my childhood kept surfacing. I vividly recalled my ninth birthday, when I blew out my candles and wished to be a pro baseball player. That was a time in my life where anything felt possible. When dreams were attainable and my ability was exponential. I would go out in the backyard every day and throw the ball around and imagine being in the big leagues. My heart was pure, and I believed in myself wholeheartedly. I never doubted myself or felt that my dreams were impossible. That energy and that kid was the most authentic form of who I was that had ever existed. However, when that spirit was crushed, it caused me to never step foot on a field. To never give it a shot. To never even try.

I started to feel depressed for giving up on the kid with illustrious dreams. For killing off the possibilities before they could even exist. It wasn't necessarily about sports or any particular memory. It was the way I'd neglected myself. This realization ate away at me. I started to think about every situation where I had defied my true self and failed to love myself and what kind of energy and outcomes that had created in my life. There were countless memories I played over and over in my head. Sports, my family, my relationships, high school, not going to college, my shattered dreams. I felt regret so intense, so powerful that it pierced to my core, to my soul. Those visions and feelings tortured me. I had deprived myself of my passions my entire life. There was a side of me that loved life, loved people, loved feeling a part of something. I loved challenging myself, I loved competition; I had wanted to experience it all. But I never tended to that side of myself long enough to allow it to exist.

I was tormented by this realization. I was sure I'd never be able to go back and live those moments I wasted. Even though it felt like my life had changed forever in the blink of an eye, it actually hadn't. My careless attitude and lifestyle took place over the course of ten years. All the while, I could have changed and decided not to live my life as I was. When I was in the midst of it, I didn't see it that way. I had always felt like a victim, a prisoner, but I could suddenly see that my choices and my choices alone contributed to the remorse I was feeling. Nothing and no one else was to blame. Once I started to connect the dots, I could see everything more clearly. It wasn't just about giving up on sports or on school, it was giving up on everything and the way I had chosen to live my life.

As I've mentioned before, the deep sorrow I endured those first couple of months of my incarceration sparked something inside of me that I desperately needed. It was something I'll never forget, and it changed my perspective forever. I felt cheated and betrayed. Not by society or my parents but by myself. But instead of dwelling on the fact that I had wasted so much of my life, I became obsessed with redemption.

I felt a genuine desire to live my future in alignment with my true self. To seek true meaning and purpose within my life. To make unforgettable memories and experience love, joy, and excitement to its fullest. I made that solemn oath in those moments that I would never breathe life into the inferior version of myself ever again. I knew that, despite all that I neglected and would never get back, I could still redeem my actions from then on out. I still had enough time to make something of myself. I could still live a fulfilling life that I loved. I didn't even know what that was at the time or what the future held for me or even how much time I would spend in prison. However, I did know that, no matter what, I would never ever experience that regret again. No matter what!

This is when I first experienced what it meant to be "free." What it truly felt like to be content, whole, and sound. It all derives from within. It wasn't freedom in the physical realm that I was seeking. It was inner peace and gratitude that I had been searching for my entire life, the emotions I had been detached from for so long—love, joy, and desire. I was starting to feel alive, and it was incredible.

These thoughts and feelings became the driving force behind all my actions from that moment onward. It didn't matter what I was doing, I would give my all to everything and anything I did. Every pushup, every letter, and action would be done to the best of my ability with all the attention, effort, and care it required—because that's what every moment meant to me now that I was able to feel gratitude and love for life. Through every little action, moment to moment, I would put forth my best. That's what it would take. Eventually, this mentality grew and expanded to create a reality I never could have fathomed. However, if I was to fully embody this mindset and state of being, first I had to permanently eradicate anything that could hold me back.

For months, I went back and forth from the county jail to court. They were long days where I was shackled up sitting in holding cells, lost in thought while the other inmates talked amongst themselves. I chose to keep to myself as much as possible. I noticed that I was starting to feel repelled by the dialogue and energy I felt in those holding cells. I could see clearly how ignorant and limiting the mindset and lifestyle I once displayed truly was. Most of these guys weren't necessarily bad people, just lost or confused like I was. It became more and more evident to me how destructive the old behaviors, addictions, and codependent relationships I had once glorified were.

I was in this continuous process of reflection, like a trance or hypnosis, more hours of the day than I could count. I had stopped paying attention to the court proceedings or my case after the first month. Every time I was brought into the courtroom I would see my lawyer and the district attorney laughing and making small talk. I noticed the way the judge looked at me while the officers escorted me in. Everything was merely a formality at this point, with the overwhelming consensus that I was guilty. There was nothing I could do to change anyone's opinion of me. Instead, I continued to peer within for guidance and strength to persevere.

I'll never forget one day at court when I was one of the last to be seen by the judge. I sat in a holding cell from 6 a.m. to 4 p.m., cuffed up just to be told to come back next month, so I could do it again. That happened all the time, but I had stopped getting frustrated. I didn't feel that it was even worth wasting energy over. I could only focus on the aspects of life that were under my control. On this particular day, I was alone in my holding cell waiting to go back to court. I was still coming to grips with my situation and rehashing all the mistakes and wrong decisions that had led me there. As I sat ruminating, thinking about the day's court proceedings, my uncertain future, visions, and distant memories from my past, a powerful thought struck me. "I don't ever have to use drugs or alcohol ever again."

Very subtle but matter-of-fact, this realization rocked my world. I had never felt this way before, let alone believed such a possibility was true. For so long, I had used drugs and alcohol as my crutch to cope. This was a life-changing epiphany; I didn't need to hide or numb myself any longer. I could face my pain, my shame, and my regret. I was strong enough. I was courageous enough. ... I was enough, just as I was. It was the first time I had felt such a notion since childhood, since that kid who aspired to be a professional baseball player. With nothing, I discovered I had everything.

I didn't need drugs or alcohol! It wasn't a question I needed to mull over and ponder further. It was a declaration! A deep and internal commitment I made to myself that, *No matter what, I would never use drugs or alcohol ever again*! To do so would be equivalent to death in my eyes. I had come so far in such a short time. I had uncovered so much about myself and about my life that had been a mystery before. Just as I couldn't relate to the guys in the holding cell, I could no longer entertain negative thoughts or my old beliefs. This was a part of my growth that I knew was essential. It was as if I was evolving before my very eyes, shedding layers from years past. This was one of the most freeing feelings and experiences of my life. On that day, in that moment I freed myself from my insidious addiction that had overwhelmed and plagued my life. I have been sober ever since and haven't craved drugs or alcohol once.

I started to feel more and more alive. My mind, my body, and my soul were all connected and existing harmoniously. I knew, before I even went to prison, that what I had uncovered was priceless, that no matter how many years I would be incarcerated, it was worth it. What I had found within and could experience in any set of circumstances at any time was invaluable. It was as if my entire life I could only see in black and white and now I was seeing colors. Only I wasn't merely seeing with my eyes, I could feel and connect with my heart in a way that I felt to the depths of my soul. My salvation had come.

I was happier in the county jail, alone and isolated, than I had been a majority of my free life. This energy that was coming alive within me started to radiate outward. Officers, inmates, and even my family members started to notice and remark. When I would write letters home or talk to family members on the phone and describe what I was experiencing, they probably thought I was crazy.

While everyone expected me to be depressed and full of despair, I would shock them with optimism and genuine gratitude. I could tell they were incredulous, and I didn't blame them. This was an uncanny situation to say the least.

Uncle Mike came nearly every weekend, and I looked forward to our time to converse immensely. One visit he looked at me and said, "This is the most I've seen you smile since you were a kid." That was one of the greatest moments of my life. He knew me better than anyone else, and he was always there to remind me of who I truly am: the kid running around the baseball field who was so in love with life. He never gave up on me even in my darkest moments. I had felt so bad during all those years of my struggle because it had driven us apart. I was never around, and when I was, we didn't connect like before. To hear him articulate exactly what I was experiencing was everything to me. I wanted more than anything to show him my true self and for him to know I was OK. During my time in the county jail, we shared more time together and more conversations than we had in the past decade. He would always tell me "You're back" or "This is who you really are. This is the true Sean." It brings tears to my eyes to reflect on those moments.

Uncle Mike was the one who instilled in me all that positive energy and love that I was able to tap into when I needed it most. It was the joy and love for life that he helped me to cultivate in my earliest years that resurfaced and brought me back to life. Words alone could never describe the gratitude I have for my Uncle Mike. "You're back, Sean. You're back," he told me again and again.

THE START OF MY TRANSFORMATION

Intuitively, I understood that I had to forgive and let go of all the pain I held onto if I wanted to keep making progress. I wasn't an angry person by nature, but I had acted like one over the years. However, I was starting to understand that I didn't have to keep myself stuck in this negativity any longer. It happened almost by chance in a thought that came to me one day. "I should write letters to my parents and forgive them for everything." I was compelled to confront everything I was still upset about. I didn't want to be hurt any longer. I didn't want to hold on to those negative emotions. The burden to do so was costly, and I couldn't sustain it anymore.

So, I decided every painful memory and traumatic experience had to be recalled. Every moment of horror had to be addressed. I had to create a different conclusion internally. I could no longer keep myself in that victim mentality, stained by guilt and shame. I had to relive those memories and create a different outcome altogether, one focused on acceptance and forgiveness rather than denial and resentment. If I couldn't do this, I could never move on in my life. I could never fully embrace the peace and self-love I could feel awaiting me. This was a necessary step to fully embodying the kid at heart—my true and authentic self. I had to heal to move onward.

Initially, I thought I would write letters of forgiveness to my parents so they wouldn't feel bad or guilty about my imprisonment. I assumed they felt a tremendous amount of guilt for the path I'd taken in life. I wanted them to know it wasn't their fault. I felt compelled to convey that message to them. Their actions had a significant impact on me; however, I could no longer remain a victim. I had to take action to break free. I had spent so many years being angry, and I didn't want to poison myself with negativity any longer. Being stuck in a negative mindset is like being internally imprisoned by your own accord. We can break free at any moment, but we either don't believe it's possible or we don't know how it can be done. I couldn't even understand this when I was in my adolescence. I was in a reactionary state that made it impossible to conceive let alone act upon this truth. But now I had all this time to ruminate, and in doing so, the answers started to appear for themselves. I had no idea how life-changing writing those letters would be.

It turned out, the process was actually for me. I was the one who would benefit the most. The emotions that surfaced felt so therapeutic. Having the opportunity to express myself, pause, and reflect, then continue writing was powerful. The memories and their emotional attachments slowly started to unravel. Piece by piece, letter by letter. The more I wrote, the more emotion was released. I could feel the tension within subsiding as I wrote. I could feel something deep within shifting. Over the course of my incarceration, I wrote more letters than I can remember. Each one helped me in different ways. When I first started, it was helping me make peace with my past.

In retrospect, I was writing to my fourteen-year-old self who had just entered high school. The kid who felt abandoned and had his world turned upside down. I couldn't change the past or what had happened through these letters, but I could help that person heal and let go of the pain once and for all. I could change my emotional response. For years, I had been stuck in the past because I couldn't accept what had happened. I was unconsciously reliving those horrible emotions day after day, living as the boy who was ashamed of his parents and devastated by their actions. I had refused to face it for so many years. Despite doing my best to stay numb, I was still identifying with that same wounded individual in many ways. The behavior I displayed proved it. It was a vicious cycle stemming from the pain I couldn't heal and it had warped my perspective.

Two transformative energies had come alive that changed my life forever: resolution and creation. I had been courageously facing my pain from the past and feeling less and less weight upon me because of it. As all of this was occurring, I realized I had to internalize a different program altogether—a renewed mindset and empowering self-image in order to approach my life differently and create new outcomes. First I had to envision what I truly wanted, and then I could embody the person I needed to be in order to turn that vision into reality. And that's exactly what I was doing. I was discarding the parts of me that weren't genuine, and I was connecting with my authentic self. I was fearlessly searching within, peering to the depths of my soul for the answers that could transform my life forever. Everything was shifting within and I knew my life experience was no longer a burden that would hold me back but a road map, a master plan, to help me navigate the future and cultivate a life I would love and cherish.

The amazing thing is that this wasn't some massive shift or event that changed everything for me overnight. It was simply my willingness to finally face things, to take time to reflect and think on a much deeper level that started to change my mentality. It was as simple as me just giving time and energy to actually face my pain.

This was just one of many life-altering breakthroughs I experienced in that cell, which ironically served as my safe haven. A place I could heal; a place I uncovered the truth, and a place I connected to myself in a way I never had before.

Late at night, when it was dark and quiet, I would feel a powerful energy stirring within. I would dream with my eyes wide open. In those moments, I wasn't even incarcerated. Grandiose and extravagant visions, as well as normal scenarios, became my escape. I started to see all the possibilities, and for the first time in over a decade, I believed they could come true. I was seeing myself as a free man with a family, envisioning what I could accomplish with sobriety, or immersed within my community.

Thinking about living my life in such a state brought forth an immense excitement for my future. This was the first time in a decade that I had been sober long enough to feel pure emotions. I had experienced the pain and heartache; now I was feeling immense joy and excitement.

But how much could I really accomplish from prison? What could I actually hope to achieve given my circumstances? To be honest, that question never posed a threat. It never crossed my mind. I had uncovered so much to explore within that I felt I had a lifetime of work ahead of me. And ironically, a prison was the perfect place to embark upon this journey of redemption, healing, and leaving behind my limiting beliefs and negative perceptions once and for all.

I refused to feed into any negativity ever again. Instead, I focused on discovering the truth. What did I truly want? What life would I be proud to live and love like no other? What would create immense joy and fulfillment that would make each day feel like the best day of my life? What did I *have* to have? What was important? Why did I want that life? Why did I need it? I asked myself these questions a thousand times in different ways every day. The more I did, the more I shifted my outlook to one of optimism and creation. The longer this went on, the less power was given to my fear and self-doubt. I had no idea at the time these visions would grow and manifest into reality.

It wasn't all pleasant, however. There were still those sobering moments when I could feel the weight of my predicament upon me. It was such an intense situation. My family was all in shock and disbelief. After all, my picture had been on the front page of the newspaper—a grim shot of me in a jumpsuit looking guilty as could be. I actually felt guilty. I think part of me associated all my years of indifference and living in opposition of my true self as an unforgivable transgression. It made me feel like my incarceration was somehow justified. I had lived a lie all those years, and now I was being punished.

Eventually, I wound up accepting a plea deal for seven years despite my innocence. There came a point when I knew it was what I must do. It was a tremendous display of faith, now that I think about it. However, if I hadn't taken the offer from the district attorney, I would likely have spent over a decade in prison, possibly two decades. No one wins at trial, and I knew this. The conviction rate for the district attorney prosecuting me was ninety-nine percent. They had built the case strongly against me, and I was not willing to risk going to trial. Imagine going into the courtroom, shackled in prison attire with family and onlookers in the audience staring at you—knowing you're about to admit guilt and accept time in prison for something you didn't do.

It didn't feel real. I still remember the looks on people's faces. I couldn't tell if it was an incredulous look or one of condemnation. Nevertheless, I was committed, and once I made that decision, there was no turning back. I didn't look at it as though I was admitting guilt or taking prison time. I was making a deep and internal commitment to myself that I would never again live a life I wasn't proud of. From that moment on, I would live every second as my true self, pursuing my true passions and desires. This was my opportunity to make it alright. I approached this moment as if it was the opportunity of a lifetime. That mentality was everything. I was blessed not cursed.

Our minds are so powerful, more so than we can ever comprehend. In six short months, I had gone from an addict living a hopeless life with no direction to a man who felt a compelling sense of purpose. In a jail cell, with next to nothing, I realized that I had it all! My awareness became gratitude for the things I had taken for granted. I developed a keen understanding of how precious every delicate moment of life truly is. This brought forth immense joy that I was able to consistently experience despite my circumstances. It was a pure and pervasive energy that allowed me to love myself despite past failures and the way I had lived my life. From that perspective, I could forgive others who had caused me harm. Letting go of the pain and anger attached to my parents was one of the most liberating experiences of my life. As that healing process ensued, over time, the internal transformation I was experiencing flourished.

When everything you've ever known or valued is taken away in the fashion I experienced, in that moment lies an invaluable opportunity for appreciation and gratitude most could never fathom. Imagine if you loved yourself and your life the way you love your newborn child or the way you envision loving life if you had millions of dollars, nice cars, and exotic vacation homes. That's what most people, as did I, associate happiness and excitement with. I'm here to tell you, it's wrong. Those are just material things with no true value other than what you place upon them. It's misdirected want and desire; what we truly yearn for is the self-love and appreciation for life in its most basic and simplest form that I describe here. It's the realization, "I am enough." Without anything, I am still worthy and my life has meaning. That form of transcending love and energy can only be found within and will never come from external sources or temporary gratification.

At least for myself, I couldn't understand how precious life, and its infinite detail, truly was until it was all taken from me. Suddenly I saw how priceless *everything* was: conversations with loved ones, the sunshine, going for a walk, the sunset, human connection, nature, literally everything. What was happening was that I was falling in love with life.

The desire I felt was powerful. At night I would envision doing the most random things when I got out. Things I never would have considered or given much attention to previously. All my visions started to center around others and helping people or being a part of the community or something special. They were all pure and genuine visions full of love and goodwill. The gratitude and appreciation for the life I felt was magnified tremendously by the self-love that was growing inside me day after day. Self-love, appreciation for every minute detail of life, hope for the future, my sobriety, a new beginning.

When I've described my experience of incarceration to others in the past, I can tell they are almost incredulous. Surely I'm exaggerating. How could this even be? I'm about to explain in a moment, but I'd like to point out that these feelings and realizations about myself and my life have been evident in all my actions since those fateful days. My entire way of being was altered to the point that my life; my thoughts, feelings, and actions have never been the same.

This was only made possible because of God and the grand and miraculous energy enlivened within me. I'll never forget the moment I came into awareness or uttered the words aloud that shook me to my very core. Just as I described the subtle thought that pierced my mind about sobriety, so too did this thought emerge from what felt like another dimension. Only its impact and significance sent shock waves through my body to the core of my soul. The ripple effects of this poignant moment are still happening in my life today.

It was late at night and the lights had been out for nearly an hour. I lay atop my prison bunk reflecting and deep in thought, as always. I had been on such a tumultuous trajectory in my life up to this point, always feeling alone in my trials and tribulations. A specific memory stands out from only weeks before my arrest when someone I was with referred to God, and I quickly stated, "There's no God." I was so disconnected and in so much pain at the time that I had indignation toward the mere thought of God, toward anything that represented good or peace for that matter. But I'll never forget, as a thought came into my consciousness out of nowhere, I actually said it out loud. "There is a God, isn't there?" The moment those words were articulated, I felt the most invigorating and palpable energy surge through my body. It arose from the depths of my being and radiated to every inch of my body. I couldn't believe this sensation and the implications of the moment. It was in that instant that I came to know definitively that I wasn't alone, and I haven't been ever since. That moment is what made my journey through prison so fruitful. It is only because of God that what I consider to be the miracle of my personal transformation was possible.

I went to prison as a man on a mission. I had been incarcerated for eight months at this point, and those were some of the most impactful moments of my life. I was on a spiritual journey, in the midst of an internal transformation. It was magical. The way I was feeling and the thoughts I was thinking were so novel. It was indescribable.

FIVE YEARS

The ride to prison is unlike any other; it's the unknown or images conjured from movies and stories you've heard that will terrify you. You can't help but feel anxious about what you'll be thrown into. You have no choice in the matter, all you can do is maintain from within. I remember leaving the county jail around three in the morning. We drove for about two hours, all the while I stared out the window up at the stars and night sky. I hadn't been outside much in the past year, so I cherished any opportunity I had to soak up my surroundings. It was a solemn moment; I was deep in reflection, mentally preparing myself for my time in prison. I had a slight understanding of what was to come, but to be honest I was entering a world of unknowns. Sentenced to seven years in prison and required to serve 85 percent, six years. There was nothing I could do to speed up time or make that go away. I couldn't think about it and misplace my energy. Rather, I was preparing myself for the defining moments of my life.

I spent the entire first day getting processed into the California prison system. My first stop was Wasco state prison, a reception center I would be housed at temporarily before being sent to another prison, called a mainline, where I'd do my time. That's when I was assigned *AN1137*. I was just a number with no significance, with nothing coming other than what was mandated. This treatment was yet another blessing for me because it only prompted me to search deeper within than I already had. Because nothing else would save me, I was forced to tap into strength and perseverance I had never sought out before. It was my internal state and connection to self that would serve me in my most challenging times ahead.

I was alone on this arduous journey seeking my redemption; however, I never felt alone. Yes, at times, I was lonely, but I always felt connected in a way that gave me a sense of hope and purpose. Nevertheless, the first three months were filled with so much uncertainty. Just like I had in my time in the county jail, I would have to adapt to my new surroundings quickly. Everything I felt and experienced in my time in the county jail would soon be tested. All my passion and desire to live a new life was in serious jeopardy. The universe was going to challenge me every step of the way to see if I was truly worthy of the redemption I sought. All the profound realizations and emotions I had recently experienced would have to be reinforced through action if they were to persist and continue to impact my life.

Before I left for prison, Uncle Mike came for one last visit. He knew what I was up against and could sense the conviction in my voice as I spoke about my future and what I wanted for my life. He shared with me an ancient fable about "Sisyphus," a man who was condemned to push a massive boulder up the side of a mountain every day. He looked me in the eyes with a more somber look than I'd ever seen before and said, "Push that rock." This was his way of telling me it would never be easy, but no matter what, I could never quit or give up. There's not much else he could have said in that situation. My Uncle Mike had always been a very loving and compassionate man, so when I saw the intense look on his face that day, it triggered me. I knew this was life or death.

When we take our mind to that place of all or nothing and experience that fortitude within, it is powerful and liberating. There are no options or choices to second-guess and get hung up on. In my eyes, there was only one route and one way to approach my time of incarceration. I chose life in every way imaginable. This wasn't something that I could kind of do or approach with carelessness. It had to be all or nothing in every second, every word spoken, every thought pondered and action taken. When we lack that perspective and urgency in our lives, when the severity of a situation is not as extreme, we tend to approach things with a careless or indifferent mentality. For me, this was the most extreme case possible, and I had to be mentally, physically, and spiritually sound in every waking moment if I were to survive. From that, I became attuned on a completely different level than we are

.

conditioned to out here. While everyone else saw in black and white and felt on the surface level, I was seeing vivid colors, every dimension, and all the angles. This was one of many blessings that sprang from this situation.

Immediately I channeled my focus on the routines and day-to-day structure I'd worked to develop in the county jail, giving my energy to the aspects of my situation that I could control. This predominantly included reading, writing, exercise, and self-reflection. In Wasco, we were in our cells all day most days. Every so often we would get yard, and I cherished those moments. We always got out around seven in the morning, and I still recall the brisk morning air and the sunrise. The morning air was so invigorating! This was the first time in nearly a year that I had gotten out into an open space big enough to run. I hadn't run in since I was a kid, but I recall yearning for a big open space to run and feel free. It wasn't much, but the yard at Wasco was big enough to run laps and accumulate some miles. I had to wear these cheap slip-on shoes you get when you arrive and a big baggy jumpsuit, but it didn't faze me one bit. Every time we had yard, I would run laps as fast as I could then work out. When I would run, every time I'd come around for another lap, the sunshine illuminated my face. I loved those moments because I didn't even feel like I was in prison. I was in a world of my own self-reflection and gratitude. This was only the beginning for me, but I was learning an invaluable lesson: to fully immerse myself in the moment and soak up anything positive I could see or feel. This mentality is what helped me to not just endure the moments I was in, but to earnestly appreciate them. With over half a decade left in prison, I had to train my mind to block out the negativity and soak up the positive any chance I got.

However, I was not impervious to my surroundings. At times the negative energy was overwhelming and the reality of my predicament was depressing. The second night I was in Wasco a fight broke out and ended with one of the guys involved being shot in the back of the head with a block gun. A block gun shoots rubber bullets and is used to break apart fights from a distance. The rubber bullets can break bones and inflict serious injury but are not typically fatal. In this particular incident the guy shot was knocked unconscious and it appeared he was mortally wounded. This is how quickly things can escalate in prison. The individual who was shot recovered but not everyone is as fortunate. About two weeks after this incident, I was out on the yard when the sirens went off and we heard loud yelling to get down. Officers ran into an adjacent building and nurses with a stretcher followed behind. After about five or ten minutes, they emerged with a body on the stretcher and the nurses were frantically administering CPR. I recall how quiet it was; everything felt like it was in slow motion. In those moments, everyone forgets about trivial problems, the chatter and nonsense are quieted as death stares at you in the eyes. People die in prison every day. This was the first but not the last time I saw someone die in prison. It was the world I was living in now. A life taken for something no one even remembers. This was the reality I was in and why I started to take every moment so seriously. Situations like this reinforced all my desire, all my determination, and the conviction I had to persevere. It was life or death both externally and internally.

Negativity was all around, but I couldn't dwell on it. Every day I had to channel all my energy inward to feed the good that was coming alive. The epiphanies I experienced about my life wouldn't serve me unless I was able to express them entirely. I had to put those notions into motion and bring them to life through my actions. I just knew and felt that unless I lived every moment as if it was my last, I would never accomplish what I wanted in my lifetime. Think about it; I was looking at a minimum of six years left in prison with a history of no success in life and hardly any skills or assets to build upon. I knew the truth, I could see it. I had a long way to go from that cold and lonely cell to the life I envisioned and wanted so badly. It was scary and nearly impossible to achieve what I set out to accomplish. But only if I believed that. Rather than live in that fear, I sought to maximize every waking moment and create a masterpiece of my life.

This was when I started to form unyielding discipline through my daily routines. I went all in on the aspects of my life I could control. This started by waking up early before sunrise. I would get up at 4 a.m., drink my instant coffee, and just be still. I would reflect and connect with the moment. Then I would close my eyes and meditate. I would give thanks for simply being alive, and I meant it. I would envision what could be. I would fantasize about how life could be, and what I could experience and do.

Afterward, I would always read and write for an hour before my workout. My creative thoughts would flow in that early morning hour and this gave me a chance to expound upon them. I captured and wrote down ideas, desires, and images I otherwise wouldn't connect with and saved them for a time they were needed. I was developing a systematic approach to my personal development and every facet of my life was essential.

Exercise became my escape. However, it was different than when I would escape through drugs and alcohol. I wasn't numbing myself or trying to escape my reality to stay in denial. I was escaping within to build and create. It was my outlet and a way to express any negative or positive energy. With every push up, I purged negative thoughts and feelings while simultaneously envisioning the man I was creating. Every time I felt tired and drained but kept pushing, I felt my mind and body grow stronger. Soon I got to the point where I could easily do a thousand pushups and squats in my morning workout. Every pushup, every squat was symbolic—another brick laid as my foundation was being rebuilt. I fell in love with those moments because I discovered that I didn't need anything external to feel proud of who I was and who I was becoming. It didn't matter what I was doing, only that I gave my all and didn't hold back. It was the mentality and internal state I was creating that resulted in fulfillment. It was the pride and love for myself that I was expressing in my actions that created a genuine confidence and belief in myself I never had before.

After working out and cleaning up, I would always get back on my bunk feeling a deep sense of accomplishment. I loved that feeling so much. I felt like I was in complete control of who I was becoming for the first time in my life. How ironic that I uncovered and embodied such a notion in a five-by-seven prison cell with nothing.

Every day after my workouts, I wrote letters to people back home or read one of my books. I started to soak up anything and everything I could get my hands on that had a positive message or challenged me in some way. I read Tony Robbins' *Awaken the Giant Within* and *Unbroken*, a true story of Louis Zamperini, a man who was confined within a POW camp during World War II and the incomprehensible challenges he faced. It made my situation look like nothing honestly. I loved to read and felt my mind coming alive and working better than it ever had. I knew that challenging myself from an intellectual standpoint was equally important as my physical health and well-being for the growth I sought. However, this was an area I had neglected for so long. Unlike exercise and physical fitness, this was a part of myself I wasn't confident about.

It was at this time that I was faced with a massive challenge. On the surface, it would have appeared mild but every detail mattered to me. Everything I did and how I did it was a direct reflection of who I was. My entire life I had gotten in the habit of taking shortcuts or avoiding my weaknesses as if they weren't real or would disappear through my denial. On an internal level, this caused me to doubt myself and my abilities. I felt that I was less than, but in reality, I just wasn't putting in the effort.

This morning routine was like putting my armor on before battle. By doing it, I was better equipped to face the challenges that would inevitably arise. It was a spiritual battle I fought day after day. Creating this new person took immense faith. If I wasn't following through with actions daily, my faith could have easily faded away. Every day was both a test and an opportunity.

Getting up early allowed me to put all my energy and all my focus on that day only. It helped me to avoid questioning or doubting myself. I didn't get caught up in the fact that I still had 2,000 days to go and allow myself to get discouraged by that notion. In turn, I became more alive in the moment than ever before because the moment was all I had.

Since reading and writing were a part of my morning routine, I became aware of how horrible my grammar and penmanship were as I wrote letters back home. I was embarrassed when someone would write me back with little side notes giving me corrections on spelling. This was a monumental moment, not because of my penmanship or poor spelling but a deeper reflection on my character and what lengths I would go to improve my life. Would I cut corners, make excuses, and settle for mediocrity like I had in the past? I could have easily dismissed it as something I didn't need or would hardly benefit me at this time in my life. However, I knew I had to improve myself and excel in all facets of life; everything I did was a direct reflection of who I was at the core. The love of self proven through my daily actions, the pride I took in everything I did, and the mentality that was forged through that awareness was the key to my salvation. I could feel that truth burning within, and I could not deny it.

One day when I was still in the county jail, I was sitting on my bunk writing a letter home. I had gotten in the habit of asking my cellmate how to spell certain words. This went on for some time until one day I asked him how to spell something, and out of the corner of my eye, I saw something fly over and hit me in the shoulder, "Look it up." At first I was upset, but I didn't say a word and grabbed the small pocket dictionary off the edge of my bunk. This was a moment of utmost importance. My entire life I had always sought out the easy way or asked for help to overcome any learning curve. I never took initiative; whether I didn't realize I could or I just didn't believe in myself, I'm not sure. However, this was such a critical moment in my growth when I realized I had to be the one who created the outcomes in my life I wanted, even if it was just a correctly spelled word. No one else was going to do it for me; no one else cared as much about my life as I did.

This was one of the first instances when I faced one of my weaknesses, and rather than accept it or ignore it, I was determined to overcome it. It might seem trivial, but I can't express how vital this moment was for my personal growth and how I would live going forward. I used that little dictionary to memorize thousands of new words and that consistent action gave me more confidence and positive feelings about myself and what I was doing than I can describe. It was symbolic of my journey; in a place with very little I had found something that represented hope and offered an opportunity to improve myself. I kept that pocket dictionary my entire time in prison, right next to my bunk wherever I went. And I still have it to this day, beaten up with pages falling out but still as true and sound as ever.

In Wasco, I spent hours every day reading and writing. In the past when I came across words I didn't know the meaning of, I would just assume the true definition using the context of the sentence. However, I felt that lack of effort and care would carry over into other parts of my life as well. That it would be a direct reflection of my true character. It was that serious in my eyes, it meant that much to me. This was my life; this was all I had. So I started writing down any words I was unsure of along with their part of speech and exact definition. I would go over them daily and memorize their meaning. Then every Friday, I would quiz myself on these words just as if I was back in seventh grade English class.

Furthermore, I started to incorporate these new words and my expanding vocabulary in all my letters back home and even when conversing with other inmates. It wasn't long before I was getting letters back with comments about my writing. I even had someone question whether I was writing the letters or had my celly do it! I would take time to write those letters out flawlessly with perfect grammar and penmanship. Every little detail mattered, and everything I did had to be to the best of my ability. The feeling I got, the confidence that was born within when I saw how quickly my effort improved a part of my life that I had struggled with was amazing. These small daily wins were everything to me. I finally felt good about who I was and what I was doing. I was proving to myself who I was and who I could be! Every day became an opportunity to build upon that notion.

Up until then, I had had a negative perception of my intelligence. I never applied myself in school, and over the years, I developed a belief that I wasn't smart. I had good social skills and street smarts, but when it came to my formal education, I was lacking. This belief was reinforced when I received comments about my poor spelling in letters back home. However, as I started to apply myself and improve in these areas, my thoughts on the matter did too. Up until then, I was very narrow-minded and felt as though my perspective and beliefs were concrete and static. I never thought it was possible to change parts of ourselves such as attitude, perspective, or intelligence. You hear people say, "It's just the way things are," and I believed that. However, so much of my thinking and way of living was being challenged at this time. As I started to learn new words, read more books, and improve my writing, I could envision my future self as someone who was intelligent and articulate. I then channeled this person into all my letters. When people responded positively, that reinforcement gave me tremendous confidence going forward. It wasn't that I was dumb or inept, I just hadn't been applying myself in these areas. However, when I did apply myself and put forth effort, I could produce the results I wanted. It wouldn't just happen though, I had to make it happen!

In my three months in Wasco, I did everything I could to stoke the internal fire that first ignited in the county jail. Physically I was running longer and faster than I ever had in my life. I was doing calisthenics and pushup routines in my cell every day that had me in the best shape I had ever been in. My writing, grammar, and punctuation had all improved drastically, and the confidence that I started to experience in my abilities was growing. I was feeling proud of the person I was becoming.

What's fascinating about my time in prison that I naturally started to gravitate toward all the things I had previously neglected in my life. I was looking within myself daily with honesty and open-mindedness. Having open and honest conversations with myself had a massive impact on my mental health. My thoughts and attitude became increasingly optimistic. I started openly talking about my dreams and desires for the future without worrying about what others thought or doubting myself and dwelling on the possibility of failure. I was dreaming so big and feeling all the emotions as opposed to keeping myself numb and ignorant of life's possibilities. Exercise, education, reading, writing. I didn't have to do those things, I wanted to! I developed a passion for personal growth and development in all facets of my life that was transforming the way I felt and the way I lived.

If you're reading this, I want you to understand how important this next concept is for fulfillment and success within your life right now. I was doing something at this time I had never done before in my life: I started to take massive and consistent action. Massive action doesn't mean you need massive achievement or success overnight to be successful; it's a mindset and state of being. Any action, no matter how small or seemingly insignificant, became an opportunity in my eyes. I wouldn't overthink things or question myself, I would just go for it. This approach was powerful. For one, I started to prove to myself through those daily actions who I was and that I was capable. It felt amazing to just let go entirely of any negative thoughts or limiting beliefs and start living fully as the person I aspired to be. And it started with simple actions. Over time, I was forging a discipline in myself through my daily routine that would prove invaluable. Every day I was breathing life into this new identity, and I felt myself changing and growing rapidly.

One day I decided to do something I'd never done before: write out goals for my future. I'll never forget that moment. Not specifically because of the goals themselves but because of how I felt doing it. I wasn't holding back, I was dreaming big and thinking on a grander scale than ever before. I thought of all the areas of my life I could improve and all the experiences I wanted to have. I wrote out goals and made a bucket list so grandiose it still puts a smile on my face to think about it this day. It was symbolic in many ways of my rejuvenated take on life, my second chance.

This illustrated how drastically my mentality had shifted just in this short time. My bucket list consisted of things like swim with sharks, run with the bulls in Spain, attend the opera, skydive in Hawaii, travel through Europe. It was largely adventurous, a true depiction of my mind expanding and the understanding of all the beauty that had been omnipresent yet overlooked in my lifetime. I just thought of the most exhilarating, unforgettable experiences I could fathom and wrote them all down. I just wanted to see and experience everything and anything I could.

The two major goals I wrote down for when I was released were to earn a master's degree and complete an Ironman triathlon. I remember thinking that I just wanted to push myself in all areas of my life to be the best I could. A master's degree, in my eyes at the time, would be a major challenge and accomplishment. I had never considered pursuing a degree in higher education before, and the mere fact that I was motivated to do so and believed I could was in itself an accomplishment. The Ironman was something I read about and I remember thinking it seemed impossible: swim 2.4 miles, cycle 112 miles, and run 26 miles in that order successively. I could hardly imagine doing that, but I wrote it down anyway. These two goals were very important to acknowledge because earlier in my life I would have limited myself with doubt and defeating thoughts. I would never talk about these things or act as if I could do them. Now I was writing them down, thinking about them, and telling people I was going to do these things. I was envisioning what I could experience in my lifetime, free of restraint or limitations. I realized there was no harm in imagining these amazing accomplishments, but it would be detrimental to limit myself by not believing in what I could achieve. I allowed my thoughts to roam freely, and I explored all of the whimsical desires that flooded my consciousness day by day.

It was like a microcosm of worlds and endless opportunities were upon me. I could explore these amazing new thoughts and feelings free of self-imposed judgment or my old limiting beliefs. It was such a liberating experience because, for all those years, I thought it was my parents or the drugs or my environment that was holding me back. But in reality, it was me all along. It was my negative self-image, my self-doubt, my fear. I started to understand it all, and I realized I could let go of all the things that held me back in life. I could think, act, and be different. Not just a little bit, but all the time, forever! I used the habits and routines I forged early on in my incarceration at every new prison I went to.

I remember thinking, "What better place than here?" If I could sustain this mindset and behavior there, imagine what I could do when I got out. That internal belief fueled me. Every day my surroundings were in complete contrast to what I stood for and who I wanted to become. It was perfect. It was a constant reminder of what was at stake. Every time the keys jingled or I heard cell doors shutting, each morning when I opened my eyes to fluorescent lights and stainless steel, all the foul smells and distinct sounds, it all reminded me of my wasted years. I can't describe to you how motivated and inspired I felt daily. When I say I was a man on a mission, that is no fabrication.

An amazing step in my transformation occurred when I heard about a college correspondence program offered at some prisons. I found out I could actually get a college degree while in prison, and that I wouldn't have to wait until I was out. With my newfound mentality, the thought of earning a college degree while incarcerated inspired me, and I was determined to make the most of it. Discovering that my time in prison could be externally productive as well as internally created incredible excitement within.

Getting up early, looking up words in the dictionary, exercising, taking pride in who I was and how I was living in every moment no matter what I was doing—those baby steps were all building blocks. The confidence I gained from taking those actions prepared me for bigger opportunities that could propel me forward. This is one example of how the energy and mindset we cultivate moment to moment in all the little things we do ultimately prepare us to seize life-changing opportunities when they come our way.

When I enrolled in college, I decided to major in psychology and business. I sought out two degrees because I wanted to learn as much as I could and felt both those subjects would benefit me when I returned home. I went all in and was determined to be the best student I could be.

I fell in love with my courses and education in general. I had been craving that opportunity all along but just didn't know it. I became obsessed. I took four classes per quarter and would always have my textbooks and recreational reading material on the side. Between coursework, reading novels, writing letters home, and daily journaling, I became a voracious student. I was becoming not just a student regarding my education but I was also a sponge soaking up every little detail pertaining to my life. I was becoming a student of life continuously open to growing and learning.

I continued to learn more about myself through this process; I never realized how much I loved to read and write. As I immersed myself in my studies, I felt my mind continue to grow sharper. Like dusting off the cobwebs. I became fascinated reading about topics I never would have before—biology, psychology, business, mathematics. Now there was a microcosm of worlds to explore on a daily basis. When I was deep in thought or reading about how attitudes, beliefs, and perceptions are formed in my psychology classes or the intricate dynamics of cellular functioning in biology, I was captivated. I wasn't in prison at all during those moments. I was a student in the internship of a lifetime. Every day brought forth an opportunity. Every day brought forth excitement, and I was experiencing a purpose and direction I never had before.

Yes, I was in prison, but I hardly ever felt incarcerated. I was learning such a powerful lesson about self-preservation and mental fortitude. I could have easily gotten distracted or dissuaded by my predicament. That would have led to feelings of depression and hopelessness, which would have made my time in prison unbearable. However, I chose to fixate on the upside and anything positive I could detect. This approach not only helped me feel as though my time was productive and meaningful but it helped me cultivate the energy and excitement I would need to achieve what I aspired in my life.

Even though I wasn't in a physical school, I was still required to do all the same work as anyone earning college credits. In my school, my classmates were murderers, drug addicts, and people who just didn't care. I was faced with adversity and tested in a number of ways daily. Obviously, the most challenging part was my surroundings. A big room of inmates walking around, talking raucously, arguments and drug use rampant, and there I was, at a table with books and papers spread out, immersed in my studies. That was honestly one of the most difficult things I've ever done. This created a discipline and patience component that would suit me tenfold in my future. My ability to delay gratification for something more meaningful and fulfilling became apparent. To stay true to who I was, who I wanted to be, despite distractions or all the uncertainty around me. At any time my college courses could have been rescinded due to some new rule within the prison system. Oftentimes textbooks or important coursework would be late or turn up missing. It was perfect. I didn't want it easy, I had to earn it. I had to prove it to myself. I had to keep my faith and vision alive in these trying moments. This was relevant because there are so many distractions and obstacles that can hinder us in pursuing the things we truly want in life. This goes for everyone everywhere—not just me because I was in prison. If you're at home with your kids or at the office with employees, it's all relevant. It's the internal battle we fight daily.

I had to remember in every moment why this was important. I had to believe that my actions would pay off. Every moment, every second I was faced with the choice to quit and give up. It would have been the easier thing to do, but internally it would have killed me. Every day that passed in which I persevered and stayed true to who I was, my dreams started to come alive before my eyes. I took immense pride in what I was doing and was feeling so good about myself for persevering. This pride continued to grow and eventually transcended into self-love. This form of love is so profound; it magnified my appreciation for life and inspired me to create purpose no matter where I was or what I was doing.

I took such tremendous pride in my course work and education. I didn't give myself a pass on anything. I can remember writing entire papers over and over in order to depict the perfect imagery for the concepts I was elaborating upon. It was a form of art in my eyes. It was poetry in a sense, and despite the fact that it was an educational paper, I found that, with time and focus, I could paint a beautiful picture with my words. Picture me, in a cell with papers strewn all over the place, deep in thought articulating the difference between ionic bonds and covalent bonds, or citing various psychologists and their contributions to modern psychology, while a storm raged on just outside the door. This was my safe space: my classroom, my gym, my office, my sanctuary. In my cell, I could go anywhere and be anything. When I stepped out of those doors, I carried that energy and perspective with me. I was cultivating the person I needed to be to achieve my goals and live my dreams. Every day, every minute.

One of the more rewarding experiences I had in prison came about two-and-a-half years in. I received a postcard from my "Humanities through the Arts" professor. She was appalled that I was in prison and expressed her admiration for the recent paper I had submitted. For our final assignment, I had to read a series of short stories and analyze them using critical thinking and other techniques we'd been taught that semester. I had time in my favor, and I was already in the habit of looking beyond the surface for greater meaning both in myself and my life. I spent hours dissecting the stories and articulating the subplot and various themes I uncovered. My teacher wrote to tell me that I had submitted the best paper in the school. I don't know how many classes she taught or how many students were enrolled at Coastline Community College that year, but nonetheless, it felt really good to get this type of recognition. This was very helpful to my self-confidence and self-image. Deep down inside, my entire life, I knew I could be good or even great at things if I tried. But all those years, I never tried. Here I was now, pouring my heart and soul into anything and everything I did, and I was starting to get the positive feedback that confirmed my beliefs. "I could do this." "I am enough." "I can."

While I enjoyed all of my subjects, I fell in love with psychology. Learning about the intricacies of human behavior fascinated me. At a time when I was so focused on improving myself this material resonated soundly. One of the most remarkable experiences I had in prison was studying psychology and sociology while observing the population around me. The guards, the inmates, and the teachers and staff in the prison all became subject matter. I would objectively approach each day as if I were an intern or researcher seeking to learn more about the prison population. What a fascinating approach to my days in prison! This was beneficial for so many reasons.

First, as I've mentioned before, I didn't feel like a prisoner when I was able to escape the confinement of the prison walls and explore the microcosm of psychology and how it pertained to my current surroundings. I felt more like an intern or inmate counselor than anything.

Second, it gave me great insight into a group of people and their behavior I would have never had otherwise. It helped me to seek to understand others rather than judge them. People's negative remarks or behavior didn't affect me; they were merely observations and something to explore further. I didn't make it known what I was doing or where my mind was, but everyone noticed how much self-control and patience I had. This was so powerful because prison can be a very negative and confrontational place. But I was determined to avoid altercations and make my time as productive as possible.

My steadfast approach to education resulted in four college degrees. Initially, I only sought one degree in social and behavioral sciences, but I wanted to continue to challenge myself and make every day count. This allowed me to get additional associate degrees in psychology, business, and humanities through the arts. I was extremely proud of my accomplishment. My education resulted in so much intrinsic growth. Through diligence, I transformed the way I perceived myself and the world at large. At that point in my life, this was my greatest achievement, and I had been challenged every step of the way. I had not only been working hard to overcome my surroundings and persevere but I also had been working to overcome myself as well. Fighting two battles simultaneously made my triumph all the more rewarding.

Limiting beliefs, doubt, fear, uncertainty; I crushed it all through positive action. The greatest result I could ever receive from my efforts was confidence in who I was and my abilities. That transformative energy cannot be measured; it is invaluable. When we pursue this greater purpose and seek true fulfillment and growth in our lives, the things we think are important or spend all our time working toward and talking about materialize without failure. The results come as a natural byproduct of that energy and effort. In addition to the intrinsic benefits of earning my college degrees, I was given six months off my sentence. I was extremely grateful to know that my actions, the actions I chose before I knew I'd get time off, had positively impacted my life in such a tangible way. The impact of this accomplishment was profound. I had done it! I was enough!

I then set my sights on more growth and more challenges. I listened to my intuition and sought to conquer any fears, any doubts, or areas in my life I was holding back.

For my first three years of incarceration, I was on a mission for my redemption. I blocked everything else out including those around me. I had to; it was that focus and determination that allowed me to massively transform my life in a very short period of time. I was transforming from the inside out. Given my surroundings and what I was accomplishing, I knew these results were relevant to the outside world. I knew that my mindset and daily approach to life would help me to thrive out in society and achieve anything I set my mind to when I returned home. After a thousand days of intense focus on myself, I came to a point where I was ready to share my discoveries with others. I had fine-tuned my process of self-mastery and meticulously analyzed every detail. Now the results of my approach were evident, and I knew that, if it had helped me, this process would serve others as well. It was time to give back.

DISCOVERING MY PURPOSE

At this time, service became a focal point of my incarceration. At two of the prisons I went to (La Palma in Arizona, and Chuckawalla in California), I was automatically enrolled in SAP, which stood for Substance Abuse Program. It was a six-month program centered around recovery from addiction and rehabilitation. Both times I graduated from the program, I was given a position as a facilitator or inmate counselor. In all, I spent close to three years in those programs as both a participant sharing my own story and as a facilitator working beside the counselors to help the inmate population. Whether I was sharing my past drug use and the events early on in my life that led me to abuse those substances or facilitating a lesson and running a group as a facilitator, I took my sobriety and my position very seriously. I knew this was a matter of life or death and a lot of these guys were doomed if they didn't drastically change their ways. I looked at this as a grand opportunity; if I could just get through to one person and they changed their life, it would all be worth it.

Being locked in a small room with ten other inmates who were being forced to participate in the drug program was one of the most challenging aspects of my prison time. Most of these guys were upset about being mandated into the program and had no desire to change their ways. These were scary-looking guys who were covered in tattoos and held grim expressions upon their faces. When you walked into the room, the negativity was overwhelming. Like the damp and suffocating air during monsoon season in a desert, that energy could consume you.

But, as challenging as it was, this scenario created the opportunity for me to master one of the most beneficial skills I've developed in my lifetime. The ability to completely block out negativity and fixate on positivity no matter how minute or indistinct. Rather than get annoyed or flustered by the ignorance I was living in, I sought merely to understand. I went into every situation and every conversation with an open mind. My sole objective was to learn, and in order to do so, I knew I had to suspend my own opinions, feelings, and beliefs. I was intrigued and sought to understand why these guys were so hostile and apathetic toward life as opposed to judging them with preconceived ideas. This required immense patience, and I literally had to convince myself I was a psychologist in an undercover case study and my time in that environment was extremely valuable. Imagine that!

These were the lengths I went to in order to persevere in that extreme environment.

When I reflected on my circumstances, I realized I had an amazing opportunity that I never would experience again. Not only could I strengthen my own resolve through this trying process but I would learn. I had a distinct advantage the counselors who were brought in couldn't match. I had lived amongst the inmates in the drug program. Over time, as the other counselors continued to get shunned, I facilitated breakthroughs with some of the guys who were previously hostile or careless. Eventually, I was able to turn a high-stress environment with pervasive negativity into a unique and positive opportunity. I realized that we can always create possibilities that will elevate our mood and instill hope rather than defeat ourselves with negative assumptions. I continued to be inspired to be of service, and I grew intent on helping the guys who wanted to change.

About 90 percent of all inmates were put through these types of programs in an attempt to rehabilitate. Most of them were resistant, but some were really trying to change their lives. Despite the resistance, I'd say 95 percent wanted better lives, but less than 5 percent would show it and even fewer would talk about it or take any type of action to do it. Just as I once had been, they were scared or unsure of how to go about changing. A lot of these guys grew up in extremely challenging environments, in tough neighborhoods, in gangs, addicted to drugs.

Initially, it appeared we had nothing in common. I mean, how could this blond-haired guy from Santa Barbara relate to someone from the inner city or someone with different values and beliefs? But I never thought about that or saw any roadblocks. I looked for the similarities amongst us rather than the differences. My education, my awareness, my ability to be vulnerable and transparent in sharing my life experiences all helped me to break down these perceived barriers. We may not have outwardly appeared to have much in common, but internally, the pain, the low self-esteem, the doubt, the fear—we could relate to that in each other because we had all experienced it.

These weren't situations where a lot of people wanted to share or open up. In prison, as a matter of survival, you don't want to ever appear weak in front of others, and if one were to share something traumatic from the past and get emotional, it would be perceived as weakness. That wasn't acceptable in prison. However, I felt a need to share and express myself. I truly didn't care what anyone else thought. I wanted to take as much out of this experience as I could, and if that meant talking about my past and what I experienced, I would. Outwardly, I didn't appear as someone who had gone through hardships, drug addiction, and the chaos I experienced at home. At first glance, I was judged and the other guys assumed we had nothing in common. When I started to openly share my upbringing and the things I went through, it caught the inmates and counselors by surprise. Then as I described the effect my circumstances had on me and how I turned to drugs and alcohol to cope, or how I felt lost and like a shadow of who I truly was, the other inmates could relate to me. My transparency and vulnerability opened a door for communication that never would have been possible otherwise.

I would see the guys from the program back at the building or on the prison yard, and they would give me a nod or start up a conversation. These are guys whom I normally wouldn't converse with, from different cities and from seemingly different backgrounds. But we could connect on a level most didn't recognize initially. Typically, the only time we spoke to one another was during a workout or afterward, walking in the yard. These were usually surface-level conversations with little substance, just to pass time or bridge any awkwardness. However, that started to change over time. It began with harmless questions about something I'd shared earlier that day in a group or maybe a lesson I'd facilitated earlier in the week. I would walk laps with guys on the yard or they might approach me in the building, and we just started to talk more frequently. This dialogue was the first step and allowed me to connect with these guys away from the spotlight of the group. The real breakthroughs, however, always came in the middle of a grueling workout or shortly after. The endorphins and confidence that came from those highly demanding routines provided the optimal atmosphere for deeper thinking and conversation. Every workout, every day I saw their walls start to come down. I was gaining their trust over time, and I knew it. I took these moments to heart because I knew what was at stake for everyone once they got beyond the walls.

Not everyone was open and willing to face their fears, of course. Out of ten guys, one or two might not want anything to do with me. They had their own agenda and it was apparent they wanted nothing to do with sobriety, making changes, or anything to do with my approach. That was fine. There was no ill will, and we were always respectful to one another, but that's as far as it went. Then there would be about four or five guys who were conflicted. They wanted to change and would joke about it or engage in our conversations either in SAP or out on the yard from time to time. However, they weren't ready or they were just scared of the unknown. I planted seeds whenever I spoke to those guys, but I also gave them space and I noticed they were always watching from a distance. The remainder of the guys wanted more for themselves, and they would openly express that notion. Oftentimes they just didn't know what to do or where to start.

That's when I would help them. One of the fastest and most effective ways to transform our mindset and self-image is through action. When it comes to changing our perception, our attitudes, and behaviors, just talking about it isn't enough. The guys I mentored, just as myself, had a long history of failures and self-destructive lifestyles. Before they could start to envision a new life, they needed to believe it was possible. This started by believing in themselves. No matter how faint that internal belief was initially, we had to start breathing life into that person. One of the most effective ways to generate that inner confidence was through exercise. Most of these guys were in poor physical shape and still recovering from the damage caused by drugs and alcohol over the years. Similar to my experience, living carelessly had been detrimental to their growth.

So I had them work out with me and check in throughout the day. I saw some of those guys transform before my eyes. Going from someone who felt self-conscious and appeared lost, as I once was, to exuding genuine confidence and conviction in who they were and what they wanted from their lives. It was a constant battle, but these guys showed up to fight every day, and I looked at it as my responsibility to be by their side every step of the way. They trusted me, they believed in what I stood for, and because of this, they were willing to follow my guidance.

I'll never forget how amazing it was to watch someone who felt weak both internally and externally start to come alive before my eyes. It was as if every pushup created hope and each workout they completed changed their mindset—and they got into amazing physical condition as well. Some even started taking college courses and talking about new careers or paths in life they had always wanted to explore. The ripple effect from the time and energy they invested in themselves was evident. It was inspiring. I had felt the benefits of exercise firsthand and how it positively shaped my self-image and perceived abilities. Seeing this same transformation in others, in one of the most adverse and hopeless environments imaginable, was incredibly moving.

This was a pivotal time in my personal growth. Initially, I wanted nothing to do with the ignorance that was pervasive behind the walls. I limited my interactions and stuck to my own agenda. However, that close-mindedness prevented me from seeing positive opportunities that were all around me. That attitude and approach limited me and my growth more than it helped me. My attitude and perspective started to change the more time I spent working with other inmates. Over time, I could sense a deep and unrelenting desire to serve and help others.

I knew I was on to something. It was obvious how powerful this process was. The guys who continued to invest in themselves every day and face their fears were excelling. Soon they were getting up early and challenging themselves in other areas of their lives aside from our workouts. Daily routines, reading and writing, college courses, sharing at SAP, and talking about things they'd never shared with anyone. Seeing these guys step way out of their comfort zone and start to pursue the vision of themselves they'd always wanted, that was everything. It reminded me of my first year and all the changes I went through internally that gave me life. It was an amazing feeling, as if I could relive those transformative moments through the changes they were making. It helped me never forget. In turn, I could help others while staying connected to the powerful emotions and realizations that had transformed my life. It was in these unforgettable moments that I discovered my purpose, and I knew I had gone through this experience for a reason. I knew, and felt within my heart, without a shadow of a doubt that my incarceration had occurred for a specific purpose. I was going to dedicate the rest of my life to reaching others who were afflicted as I once was and share my story with them in the hopes they could discover within themselves what I had found within myself. Since those fateful moments, I have never looked back. I'm on a continuous mission to serve and inspire everyone I come into contact with through my words and actions every single day.

When we are fortunate enough to have that sobering moment when we realize exactly what we want in life, we must pursue that vision with everything we've got. That is one of the most important messages I want to convey in this book. If you do so, it will massively transform your life for the better. You must pursue your vision rather than give voice to your doubt. Every challenge I overcame or goal I achieved drowned out that inner voice of doubt and uncertainty. Through that process, I was creating an approach to my life that felt unique and empowering. This became my personal formula, a blueprint I could execute and follow no matter where I was or what I faced. I never had that before. In the past, I had always lived at the mercy of my surroundings and because of this, my demons feasted upon my weaknesses.

Facing our fears is one of the most crucial aspects of growth and personal development. I made so many internal promises to myself when I first was incarcerated and in my first year of prison. One of the most important commitments I made was that I would put myself out there and try things that made me nervous and uncomfortable. As a SAP facilitator, I had to speak often in front of the community. I remember how nervous I was the first time. My palms were sweating and my heart was beating rapidly in my chest. I tried to calm myself with deep breaths and some positive self-talk, but I couldn't settle myself. I'd never spoken in front of crowds before, especially sharing something as vulnerable as my past and my transgressions leading to prison in front of a room full of unwelcoming prisoners.

That first speech wasn't my best. My face turned red, and I felt my voice quivering. I couldn't think clearly and felt myself repeating words and losing my train of thought. However, I got through it and felt a huge sigh of relief as I walked back to my seat. I also felt excitement and a rush of adrenaline for overcoming my initial fear and apprehension. That was the first time in my life I had put myself voluntarily in such an uncomfortable situation. I had lived in the moment and faced it. Afterward, something happened that I'll never forget. A handful of guys approached me and said they liked what I said. Throughout that day other inmates commented on my speech and gave me positive feedback. Some of them I didn't even know or had never talked to before. By being open and vulnerable, I invited them to approach me and for us to have a conversation we otherwise never would have had. Over the next two years, I constantly put myself out of my comfort zone speaking in front of the counselors and the inmate population. By the time I left La Palma prison in Arizona, I felt as though sharing my story and speaking in front of others was something I might like to do more one day. I had a message I knew could help others, and I wanted to share it. However, I was far from comfortable doing so and it's possible I would have allowed fear and my insecurities to hold me back had I not come across a unique self-help group at the last prison I was sent to.

Toastmasters is an international organization that facilitates public speaking, effective communication, and leadership skills. I couldn't believe they had a group in prison for this. The final prison I was sent to, Chuckawalla, had more opportunities and self-help groups compared to the other facilities I was at. There were more rehabilitation programs designed to help inmates and prepare them for re-entry into society. I started to attend Alcoholics

Anonymous and Toastmasters every week during this last year of my incarceration. In addition to my position as an inmate counselor in the drug and alcohol program, I had the opportunity to share and speak often in both AA and Toastmasters. In our Toastmasters group, we would actually prepare speeches and recite them in front of our peers at a scheduled meeting. This was different than speaking about addiction or my past because I wasn't just sharing about my life experiences, I was creating a speech around a specific topic with specified rules and a timeframe. It was nerve-wracking all over again. Just when I thought I'd mastered my skills in elocution, I was back to square one. In Toastmasters, we learned about timing and tonality when we speak, body language, eye contact, and how to not say "um" one hundred times as we transition from thought to thought. I had never experienced anything like it.

I was also impressed by the other inmates who participated. They were incredible, and I was shocked the first time I attended a meeting and heard their speeches. Three inmates gave prepared speeches that were seamless, eloquent, and entertaining.

During what I thought was my final speech, I finally let go of all my fears and insecurities and just went for it. It was my best speech by far and I nailed it. No missed words or broken sentences. Excellent eye contact and body language. The guys applauded, and it felt so good to get that recognition. Again there was that feeling that I'd done it. The feeling I'd been longing for all those years when I hid from my true potential through my excuses. Here I was in prison, a place built for punishment to confine criminals, and I was doing more good in my life than ever before. The most amazing feeling comes when we conquer a fear of ours and we realize how capable we truly are. In those moments it becomes evident that whatever it was that we perceived to be so daunting wasn't nearly as powerful as we allowed it to be. Those moments can be life-changing, and the more we face those fears, the more we can improve our lives. Every time we follow our heart and listen to our intuition that will inevitably lead to our higher selves, the universe responds in our favor.

It turned out I had one more speech to give and it came as a complete surprise only months before my release. One of the counselors in the drug and alcohol program approached me and asked if I would speak at an upcoming event. Every so often they would bring in outside speakers to share on a topic related to addiction or sober living after release. I assumed it would be a casual engagement, sharing as I did frequently in front of twenty to thirty inmates and some counselors as well as the outside volunteers who were coming to put on the event. I agreed and didn't think a whole lot about it afterward.

What I didn't know was that this was an important event because organizations were coming in to share their resources and opportunities for inmates who would soon be released. The prison staff and counselors at the drug program had gone out of their way to make this a big deal. Although not a lot of the guys acted as if it was important, deep down inside they all cared. The ones that really wanted to change for the better were at a severe disadvantage going back to their old neighborhoods and lives. These organizations offered alternative choices and the resources to make it possible to get a fresh start once they were released. The event looked more like a job fair than a prison event. Of course, our surroundings were the same and nearly everyone was dressed in the prison attire, but the energy was so much different.

Multiple speakers shared about their organizations and how they help inmates transition back into society. They even had some ex-convicts who had turned their lives around share their personal journeys. It was very inspiring to hear these guys recount how they changed for the better once they were released from prison. I had the opportunity to speak toward the end of the event, and I was surprised I wasn't as nervous as I thought I'd be. All the times sharing in groups, speaking in the counseling program, and participating in Toastmasters had provided valuable experience. I had never given a speech in front of this many people, around 250 including the inmates, staff, and outside representatives. The warden was even there, whom I'd never seen once at any prison I had been to in the last five years. They rarely are seen in the prison yard. This was an important moment in my life that I'll never forget. I had dedicated the past five years of my life to challenging and continuously developing myself. I was facing all my fears head-on in pursuit of this dream life I had cultivated and kept alive all these years in prison. I felt like this moment was not only a test but an opportunity to finally share this person on a bigger scale. Despite there only being a couple hundred people in attendance, and most of the inmates, I took this experience to heart.

For so many years, I had cowered behind my shadow, never wanting to be noticed or stand out. Now here I was, in the prison blues, openly sharing and expressing myself in a way I previously never would have. This was the perfect opportunity for me to step into the light, into alignment with my true and authentic self, and publicly display that person. Although it was still in prison, I was finally facing my fears and living as the person I knew I could be. A leader, a person who cares about others and loves helping people. A person not afraid to be open and put themselves out there to do what he feels in his heart is right. A person ready to use his gifts and abilities to help others.

I was proving all of this to myself and had been for the last five years. After my speech was over, it was probably only four minutes long, I was approached by both inmates and staff members. It was encouraging to hear positive feedback. My fear of not being good enough was a huge part of the reason I held myself back most of my life. The difference now was that my desire to excel and succeed in life far outweighed any fear of failure. I had shifted the balance in my favor through continuous effort. What started as a mere vision accompanied by intense desire had literally manifested into my reality. I was the person of my dreams. It was real now. That moment, it all came together and I was able to stand up—proud of who I was— in front of all those people without feeling self-conscious or fear of judgment. This was a defining moment in my life, and I would carry that message in everything I did going forward.

I heard a lot about guys who got out of prison and would come right back in. I even saw several guys who'd gotten out come back before I left. It was sad, but it happened frequently. Every so often, you'd hear about someone who was murdered shortly after their release. These occurrences were very impactful whether I'd known the person or not. Even though I wasn't in gangs or from a crime-ridden area, I was still affected. It was relevant to the internal battle I had been incessantly fighting. To me, life had taken on such a different meaning and purpose when compared to my early years. I looked at my incarceration as a rebirth of who I was. This was my second chance, and life and death were very much on my mind often. Not death in the traditional sense but on a spiritual level. I was thinking about my future, my dreams, and my redemption. I had taken my experience as if I actually died, and this was my second chance at life. I would not waste a moment.

All the hurt and suffering you've ever experienced is magnified in prison. Being deprived and away from people you love as time passes you by is a horrific existence. That's why I escaped within myself as often as possible for those 2,000+ days. I had to maintain an impenetrable mentality and relentless approach to my personal development in order to thrive. Of course, occasionally I felt depressed due to my predicament. There were days when I was caught off guard by painful news and adversity hit me hard.

One of those days was when I called home and one of my uncles told me my grandmother had passed away. Those are the most heartbreaking moments to experience in prison. My grandmother was the matriarch of our family and represented everything righteous in this world. She raised nine children, seemingly by herself, and was strong and resilient. She epitomized love, selflessness, and determination to me. As a kid, I thought she would live forever. Nothing ever fazed her. Months before my incarceration, I would often go by and see her, and I was very grateful for all the time I was able to spend with her before my arrest. I was deeply saddened by her passing, but I took solace in knowing I was close to her in the days prior to my incarceration. Her passing taught me another lifelong valuable lesson. We always think we have more time, but when someone dies, we have regrets for not taking the initiative to spend more time with them. When it's too late, there's nothing we can do. If you truly love someone, tell them often and go see them. No excuses. Whether it's a lack of time or money to travel, those excuses or perceived reasons will never comfort you in times of mourning. My grandmother was one of a kind and had a lasting effect on so many people whom she raised and cared for over the years. That day, I locked myself in my cell and cried as I spoke to her.

I wound up losing three family members while I was away in prison all in that same year. After my grandmother Mary passed away, the second one was somewhat expected as my grandfather Ron, my mother's father, had become increasingly ill over the course of my time incarcerated. My mom and I were corresponding often ever since those first letters while I was in the county jail. She had since reconnected with her parents and was seeing them more often. It warmed my heart to know she got to spend time with her dad before he passed. Although I knew it was coming, the news of his passing still stung. I hadn't seen my grandfather since I was fifteen. Death is never easy to accept. There is something deeply unsettling knowing you will never see that person again.

I was somewhat prepared for my grandfather's passing; however, I was not prepared for the news of my mother's death only months later. I was shocked and at a loss for words. She had died suddenly from a brain aneurysm. I couldn't believe it. Since we reconnected while I was in jail, she had consistently written me letters and we had mended our broken relationship. Things would never be as they were before she left us when I was a kid, but I had worked hard to let go of my resentments toward her. I always had a vision of getting out and the two of us going out to lunch and reconnecting. I thought with both of us being older and sober, we could have a renewed relationship, free of past wrongs or painful memories. It was something I thought about often, and I was devastated when I found out she passed away so unexpectedly. I isolated myself for a week to mourn and reflect in my own way.

I was in disbelief; it wasn't supposed to go this way. Everything in my life had been steadily improving, and now people were dying, and life felt cold and dark again. In the past, I would have immediately gone to numb myself and stay high as long as possible. Despite the pain I was enduring when my mother passed away, I never contemplated that as a possibility. Instead, I chose to stay to myself and mourn in my own way. I was still trying to accept that she was gone. Although she let us down when we needed her most, she was my mom and I loved her. I had so many memories of childhood in which she was the loving person I knew her to be at heart. It's a shame that her behavior later on in life distorted that image I once had. The last time I ever saw her was one of my last days in court. I was cuffed up, leaving the courtroom, and she was in the audience clearly distraught and hardly recognizable. She was crying and saddened by my predicament. It killed me to see her like that in the moment. However, what brought me immense joy was knowing that after that day, instead of going deeper into her addiction and self-destruction, she got sober and cleaned up her life. I had expected her to fully self-destruct when I went away. That year, Sara and Kevin spent Thanksgiving with my mom's side of the family. Although I never got to see my mom again, I was comforted knowing she didn't die on the street in some horrific fashion. As callous as it sounds to articulate that last sentiment, that was the truth and the reality we faced. Drugs and alcohol will poison the best of people. It ruins lives and can crush your spirit. I love my mother dearly and still shed tears to this day from time to time when I feel her presence.

All of these details, every sign that appeared from the day of my arrest onward kept me keenly aware of how precious this life truly is. Everything that took place in my time of incarceration served to keep this in the forefront of my mind. This was part of the process, part of my growth, and it ensured I would never forget or grow complacent. My redemption was all-encompassing— death, rebirth, challenges, growth, and all my deeper thoughts and emotions had converged to make this transformation possible.

No matter where you are, being prepared to deal with adversity and life's challenges is essential. In prison, if I hadn't been so immersed in my personal growth and development, I would have been derailed several times during my incarceration. That would have been the end of me. I would have been doomed. When that happens, when we encounter great tragedy in our lives or fall victim to self-defeating thoughts after a perceived failure or setback, we typically revert back to old ways of thinking and behaving. This is counter-productive and oftentimes we regress rapidly to the point where we're worse off than ever before. This was one of the reasons I'd felt so lost in my life before prison. My attitude or my actions were often reactions to some person or situation that was going on around me. In reflecting on that while I was in prison, I thought, "Wow, I've been incarcerated mentally nearly my entire life." I worked hard to gain control over myself and be completely attuned internally. So when I received bad news from home or had a tough day, I recognized that it was another test. I never would allow those moments to take away what I had created, what I'd been living and breathing life into all these years. This resulted in an unwavering mindset in the way I lived my life. I had created a new person to such an extent that there was no possibility of ever going back to my old lifestyle. Prison, hunger, depression, and even death—nothing would ever turn me back to my old ways.

Everything from the passing of my beloved family members to any milestone achievement in one of my programs—it all reinforced my desire to pursue my vision wholeheartedly and give my all to every moment I had. I was intent on leading by example for the guys around me and to continue to prove to myself who I was becoming.

The most effective way I could reinforce this belief and way of life was by consistently challenging myself and getting out of my comfort zone. So, every day I would push my body to the limit in workouts I never imagined I could do before. I had so much energy pent up inside. Just as writing was an outlet for me, exercise became a form of expression as well. It was my medicine, and the endorphin rush of completing grueling workouts gave me a high like no other. It was pure, and it never faded. By the time I left prison, I was in the best shape of my life.

Another personality trait I developed in prison was that I was always prepared to take action in the most trying and difficult of circumstances. One of the more extreme examples of how this day-to-day mentality was reinforced came on a day when outside temperatures reached 118 degrees. Rather than skip yard that day, I made it a point to go do pull-ups for one hour underneath the scorching sun. And, when it rained, if the weather wasn't too severe and we were allowed in the yard, I would run ten miles. This was motivated by pure gratitude. Something about feeling rain upon my face and being out in the elements felt so amazing. It brought me back to the same excitement and mentality of childhood.

I'm not a masochist and these actions weren't excessive in my eyes; they were absolutely necessary. Most people would disagree and say one day off wouldn't have hurt. That's exactly my point, and that's what I heard from guys around me every day. "You don't need college courses.

What are you going to really do with an AA degree while you're in prison?" "You don't need to get up at 4 a.m. Sleep in a little, you still have five years to go." "Why are you doing Toastmasters? You're never going to give speeches when you get out." "Why do you waste your time mentoring those guys? They'll never change, and you're wasting your time."

I heard it every day. It was almost as if my old doubts and fears were being channeled through these messages from the other inmates, and I was able to recognize this and use it to my advantage. Every time someone said something to question what I was doing and how I was living, it confirmed for me that I was on the right track. Honestly, if I wasn't drawing attention or getting those remarks, then I knew I wasn't doing my part. Imagine if I would have listened to those comments. Imagine if I would have listened to the voice in my head telling me to sleep in or stay inside because it's too hot. Imagine if I would have spent those five years staying comfortable and making excuses. If I had, I guarantee you wouldn't be reading these words right now. It was never about the heat or about the workout. It went so much deeper, and once I'd discovered this, no one could ever convince me otherwise.

Running in the heat of the sun or in monsoon-like conditions are opposite experiences, but these two examples are symbolic on the deepest level. There were many situations over that five-year stretch when I was faced with a choice that others might overlook entirely. It was a choice about who I was becoming and at what lengths I would take to get there. The harsh conditions I found myself in during those moments were symbolic of life and the challenges I would inevitably face going forward. Would I really let the weather and a small moment in time being uncomfortable stop me from pursuing my dreams? Never! I looked forward to those situations because every time a voice inside would try to tell me, "Oh you've been doing good, just kick back," or "You don't need to push yourself this hard every day," I took action in opposition to that voice—and I grew stronger and more connected to who I was creating. It went so much deeper for me than most people could see. While they were fixated on the external conditions and how hot or cold it was, I was immersed in a vision ten years in the future connecting the dots to that very moment and how the mentality I instilled day after day in prison would enable me to triumph and overcome countless bouts of adversity later on in life. I'll never forget the last ten-mile run I did in the rain when four other guys joined me. Two of them had never run as far and doubted they could make it, but everyone finished, and I can still recall the split-second look of accomplishment on their faces as they splashed through puddles. They looked like kids playing in the rain. In that moment, nothing else mattered because that's all we had. For an instant, they were laughing and smiling and they weren't in prison at all.

APPLYING
MY APPROACH
TO YOUR LIFE

Suffering through self-imposed adversity provides an opportunity for immense growth. Workouts that left you gasping for air and feeling like you are going to pass out or even die became coveted. Running for miles in one-hundred-degree weather was a grand opportunity to test one's grit and push past perceived limitations. One thousand pushups and one thousand squats before the sunrise while everyone else slept was a gift. It was in prison that I truly discovered the value in suffering; the value in challenging myself in extreme conditions. It was the effects I was after, and that high was grander than any other. I was learning to let go and surrender in those moments. When I felt weak and as if I couldn't run another lap or endure any more time under that scorching sun, I would pray and meditate. I always found the strength within to persevere, and every time this happened I was more connected and attuned than ever before. Two thousand plus days with this mindset and approach. EVERY DAY. You can only imagine what I was creating.

The more I cried out for guidance in my morning prayer and meditation, the more connected I felt. The longer I ran underneath the scorching desert sun, the stronger I became. Every lap was symbolic to me in so many ways. When I was exhausted and on the verge of collapsing, I always envisioned what I loved and cherished in my life. Every lap forced me to look deep within and connect to all the good I felt and desired in my life to keep me going. I pictured all my family members' faces and each lap was for them. I envisioned the person I was creating and asked myself what he would do when times get tough. Would he quit and give up or keep pushing onward? I did this every day. I knew then, when running those laps and suffering as I did, that I was going to bring this message, this truth, back home and it would change people's lives. All I had to do was keep it alive and continue to harness it day after day.

And this is how I did it, through this exact process I'm describing in these pages. This is the exact approach that will massively transform anyone's life anywhere. This is the approach to life and mindset that brought my dreams alive before my very eyes. I looked beyond my setting of prison; I took extreme action, and I made sure to live my life with intention and care. I focused on small details, consistency, and the subtle changes I made day to day that added up over time. It is always the deeper message where the transformation occurs.

That approach is what helped me overcome countless challenges, thrive in adverse situations, and now, I watch as others do the same—overcome alcoholism; save their marriages; take care of their health and lose forty, fifty, sixty, or even one hundred pounds; and even thrive through a pandemic when everyone else is panicking and derailed. This is the secret. I'm sharing it with you, so you can apply it too and do what it takes to live the life of your dreams. It *is* possible. And it all starts with that first step.

MY LAST DAY IN PRISON

Getting out of prison is one of the best feelings in the world. I had worked relentlessly to get to that moment for over five years and now it had come. I tried my best to stay calm and even ran a half-marathon with some of the guys the day before to ease my nerves. Nevertheless, I could hardly contain my excitement. It was surreal; my prison experience had been such a pivotal time in my life. I had been so immersed in those moments behind the walls, and now everything was about to change.

It felt as though my entire life had come down to these unforgettable moments. I was ready to bring this energy and new perspective back home to the world. I had literally transformed before my own eyes, and I was eager to share this person—not just with my immediate family or my community. I had a vision and an undeniable feeling within that was calling to me. I was excited to pursue my dreams and live life the way I knew I could. I had spent so many nights reflecting on my bunk staring out and envisioning life after prison. "What would it be like?" "How would I act?" "Are people going to accept me?"

Interestingly enough, my thoughts were very similar to those I had while in the county jail. It was the same uncertainty brought forth by the unknown and circumstances beyond my control. I had become very adept and even comfortable in the prison environment. I learned how to manipulate the variables in my favor and maximize the time I had behind bars. Now I was leaving that predictable lifestyle to explore the unknown and pursue my greater vision. It was scary, exciting, and somewhat of a mystery how I'd assimilate back into the world. However, this time, I could handle the change, because this time I was drastically different. From the time I was arrested to now, I had spent nearly six years proving who I was and living as that person. There was no doubt or question in my eyes. I was locked in and utterly transfixed by the mission and adventure coming my way.

There had been so many nights I thought about my life beyond the walls, sitting on my bunk with headphones on, looking out at the dayroom. In prison, you can get a CD player and certain CDs, and I would listen to nearly anything I could get my hands on. Ironically, I always ended up with some emotionally charged CD, something I never would have listened to before, and it would stoke a powerful energy within. I often sat in deep reflection, just as I had all those nights in the county jail, wondering what would come of my life. Here I was nearly six years later. I had done it. I had done it! I felt a mixture of deep gratitude and an immense sense of accomplishment for what I had done to turn my life around. Every moment, every decision, every action. I had faced my fears and followed my heart every step of the way, and by far, that was one of the proudest moments of my life. I had stayed true to myself in the most stressful and extreme case possible. Now, I would face a new challenge, but the mentality I had forged gave me hope.

Would I find the woman of my dreams? Would I have children? Would I follow my heart and the passion to help others I felt within? Would others believe in me and my ability to lead them? Would my message be received by those who needed to hear it? Would all my lessons and understandings help others change their life as they helped me? Would I continue to face my fears and pursue my vision? Would I lose that spark and forget everything I learned? Would I settle for mediocrity? Would I accept anything less than the best for my life?

So many questions, so many thoughts flooded my mind on those memorable nights. My emotions were a mixture of pure desire and determination blended with the uncertainty brought forth by the unknown. I knew what I wanted, and I was unwavering in that truth. However, I had never lived in that world as this man, and deep down within, the same fear and self-doubt that plagues most of us our entire life was working hard to gain control. Even after nearly six years of intense focus and effort, those same feelings that kill dreams were present; they would always be present. However, I was not the same. I was no longer weak and compromised. I had chosen positive energy. Through our actions, we reinforce the energy that controls our lives. Every day we have a choice between good or bad, positive or negative. Those choices are what shape our reality over time and affect how we think, how we feel, and how we live our lives. Despite the doubt or fear always being there, I had reinforced all the positive for more than 2,000 days, and the morning they called my name for parole, I was ready.

The day of my release, I was overcome by energy and emotion. One chapter of my life was coming to a close, while another was only beginning. I was completely caught off guard by the chain of events that morning, but it felt like a perfect ending to my life-changing journey. I got up early as usual. Time stood still while I waited to be called for parole and escorted from the building to the front of the prison. The clock ticked, and I could hear the echo of the second hand throughout the building. Second by second, nothing happened. It was dark and quiet. I was alone in anticipation of this day I had dreamed of for so long. As the sun slowly began to illuminate the building, I could hear others stirring awake. Then a thought snapped me out of my reverie. "I should already be gone!" Surely they knew it was my release date, so why hadn't they called me to the front yet? Typically anyone who is paroling leaves the building hours before sunrise. For a moment, I felt a pang of concern that they got my release date wrong or something was off. No way this could be happening! But, what was actually happening was exactly what was supposed to happen—just like my arrest and subsequent incarceration for a crime I didn't commit, it was all a part of a grand and master plan I had only recently come to recognize over time. Everything is connected, everything has meaning and purpose. At times we don't understand this, but it's always true.

I eventually was called to the front gate about an hour later. It was time! Walking out of that building for the last time was going to be one of the greatest feelings in the world. I was about to be released from prison. The anticipation, the excitement, the energy was palpable. However, when I got to the gate that led to the front of the prison, I ended up waiting for another hour. What was going on? You can imagine the thoughts racing through my mind. That hour felt like an eternity. Soon I heard them calling the buildings out for chow. I thought this was a bad sign because that would mean all the officers would be busy, and I would be waiting even longer. The morning seemed to drag on forever. In retrospect, it was as if I was meant to have that extra time. I couldn't see it yet, but this was the perfect way to end my stay in prison. It was symbolic on so many levels.

With my awareness piqued and all my focus centered on getting out, I needed to have time to reflect on my journey. To soak in every memory and lesson I'd learned the last five years. To imbue those transformative lessons and universal truths into the depths of my soul.

As I stood at the exit gate waiting for an officer to escort me to the front of the prison, the first building was let out for breakfast. When everyone started walking past me, I stayed quiet, not wanting to draw attention to the fact that I was getting out, and they were going to eat slop for breakfast. When someone paroles, it's typically met with hidden resentment and jealousy by other inmates. Everyone wants to go home; everyone is afflicted by this way of living. So I did my best to keep to myself in that moment. But then, as the guys saw me, I started hearing them yell over. I kept hearing "Captain America," as they often called me because of my blond hair. I can't remember how many guys yelled over to me and wished me well or said something positive. This went on for at least thirty minutes as the inmates from all four buildings walked around the track to the chow hall. I felt so grateful and humble in that moment. To have so many people, some who never show emotion or say positive things to anyone and some who I didn't even know, show me that respect and share their congratulations with me. I'll never forget that moment. I had never seen more than a couple people wish a paroling inmate well. Here I was, getting to receive such messages from four buildings at once with hundreds of guys.

This reinforced an understanding I still have to this day: People are always watching, whether they say so or not. If I could have this impact in prison, imagine what I could do once I returned home. I had felt that in my heart, but experiences like this one and giving the speech in front of the prison, my daily interactions as an inmate counselor, and mentoring guys on the yard solidified that notion. This is what I was meant to do and who I was. And I had been living every moment of every day as that person. The universe confirmed what I felt in my heart all along.

For the first time, I would be living in the free world with purpose, and I had all the tools, abilities, and confidence I needed to do anything I wanted in my life. And possibly even more important, for the first time in my life, I knew exactly what I wanted to do.

I had envisioned that moment more times than I could count. As soon as I was out of those prison blues, I knew it was official. I put on the Nikes my brother had sent in, and I was ready. I'll never forget the vivid colors strewn across the morning desert that day. I stepped out of a black and gray prison and into the resplendent light of my freedom. It was like a kaleidoscope of radiant colors, all so potent and awe-inspiring. I hadn't seen so much beauty in one instant, and it was overwhelming. Not in a bad way, in the most glorious of ways imaginable. The colors I was seeing and the intensity with which I felt them were perfect depictions of the peace and love I felt within. It was as if all of the emotions, passion, and desire I held on to for all those years were purged from my being. I was finally seeing what I had been feeling internally all along. I let out a howl that echoed across the vast desert landscape.

The first person I saw was my sister. I was so awestruck by the dazzling colors and majestic sunrise that I could hardly make out her face. All I could see was a silhouette and her beautiful blonde hair blowing in the breeze. I'll never forget that moment. She looked so beautiful, and as we came closer together, I could see the smile on her face. The moment was powerful. After all those years, here I was. I had made it. I could hardly believe it. Sara and Kevin were there to pick me up, and it was a perfect way to start my journey back home. During the car ride out of the desert, I held my head out of the window and just let all my emotions pour out. I had been holding so much in over the years. Despite being very attuned to myself and having done so much personal development while incarcerated, this was a different feeling altogether. Tears of joy streamed down my face as I yelled out to the desert landscape and thanked God for everything I'd been blessed with.

RETURNING TO
THE OUTSIDE WORLD

It was a picture-perfect day, and the first thing we did was drive to Huntington Beach in Southern California. The sun was radiant upon my first glance of the mighty Pacific Ocean. The water had that turquoise blue hue to it that reminded me of childhood. There were so many colors and details to take in. I looked closely at everything and soaked in the view and the deeper meaning behind every moment. It was strange to be on one of the most iconic beaches in the world when only hours ago, I had been confined to a prison.

The waves were massive, crashing hard upon the sand, which stretched as far as the eye could see. As we were walking down the boardwalk, we came across a little hut that had a sign "surfboard rentals." Suddenly my brother and I looked at each other and, without any prior arrangements, decided to spontaneously surf some waves. There I was, only hours out of a five-year prison term about to paddle out in eight-foot-high waves at

Huntington Beach! I couldn't believe it. This was all too perfect.

The first wave I caught brought me right back to childhood. I stood up, and a surge of energy flowed through my body just like when I was a kid. I smiled in that moment, realizing it was that same love and excitement I experienced all those years ago in childhood that I had taped back into while I was incarcerated. One glaring difference from those moments spent in prison and being out in the ocean was that now my surroundings mirrored what I felt within. I paused to reflect as I sat beyond the crashing waves, looking back at the palm trees and feeling the ocean mist spray upon my face. The energy of the ocean was magnetic and the smells and sights were mesmerizing. The sense of relief, gratitude, and accomplishment I felt was invigorating. That love and energy were precisely what I was determined to share with others throughout the world.

That first twenty-four hours were a whirlwind of emotions. It was amazing to be back with my brother and sister. It's hard to put into words the joy and excitement I felt. There was so much to take in, it was overwhelming in some ways. I was doing my best to readjust. I'd spent half a decade living in a very predictable environment with specific routines that never faltered. Now everything was moving fast, and it all seemed out of control. I had to focus on staying poised and embrace it all without letting the distractions rattle me and take away from the moment.

You would think that the first day or week out of prison is pure bliss; however, with so many emotions surfacing, it's almost more uncomfortable than enjoyable. I had anticipated this, but it's hard for others to understand entirely. I was grateful beyond measure, nevertheless. I had the support of my loved ones upon returning home, and that made my transition back into society easier than it would have been otherwise.

I had arranged to stay with family. Throughout my sentence, I'd communicated frequently with loved ones through phone calls and letters. They were always there for me—my siblings and all my aunts, uncles, and cousins offered a tremendous amount of support when I needed it most. Mike, Sara, Kevin, Mark, Kim, Jeanne, Rich, Beau, Trisha, Dan, Austin, Olivia, Nicole, Courtney, Dylan, Rhys, Forrest, Casey, and Kieran. My love and gratitude for them are immeasurable. Six months before my release, I reached out to my Aunt Kim and Uncle Mark, who I had been very close to growing up. They agreed to let me stay with them when I got out. Rather than go to sober living or a halfway house like most guys did, I was grateful for the opportunity to stay with my family, who offered unyielding love and support. In the past, I'd always put myself at a disadvantage with poor surroundings and bad influences. But I knew I had to put myself around the best people in the best environment I could find this time. There was no room for error.

I vowed to keep anyone I'd spent time with prior to my arrest who was still living recklessly at a distance. This included family. This was my second chance at life, and I would not jeopardize it for anyone. I would be with people I loved surrounded by natural beauty. Their property was tucked away in a canyon amongst foothills and a beautiful stream. It was the perfect place to reconnect.

I also had a good job waiting for me upon my return: working for my Uncle Mark's tree service. I had worked for his company right out of high school, and I was able to jump right back into work. I had an opportunity to grow within his company and provide a good life for myself.

Despite my tranquil environment and employment, I was out of sorts the first couple of weeks back home. I was doing my best to adjust, but I felt off. I felt alone and out of place. Not for lack of love or support, I had that in abundance. I realized I was used to always being around people. Even if we weren't talking to one another, I'd constantly been around at least one other person for the better part of five years. I found myself longing for connection and wondering about my future. I couldn't even describe what I was feeling entirely. I had a deep yearning and desire to experience something I was missing. Despite being overjoyed to be back home and out of prison, I started to feel a void almost immediately upon my release. I had overcome one challenge and now another loomed large: rebuilding my life.

By now I was twenty-nine years old, and things had changed. Everyone was married and having kids, and I often questioned whether that would happen for me. All my doubts and concerns would surface late at night as I lay awake reflecting on my life. It felt familiar. It was the same predicament I encountered those first months in the county jail or the final months of my incarceration. It was that same deep and fearless introspection and the desire stirring within that I couldn't ignore. The answers would come to me in those moments in the form of thoughts and visions, and I would meditate on them for hours. I was experiencing another internal shift. My surroundings had changed, but the same ineffable energies were stirring within. When we have these visions or desires to live our lives a certain way, we must listen to that intuition and follow our heart. To do otherwise is to go against our dreams, and we can never find the fulfillment we're seeking in life when we live in opposition to our innermost purpose and desire.

One desire was for a family, which has always been important to me. Prior to returning home, and even more so after my return, I thought about it often. I wanted a wife and children so badly to create unforgettable memories with. At this point, I was lonely despite being surrounded by people I loved. I felt a constant longing. I yearned for a family of my own that I could love and cherish. My past failures and neglect of relationships had resulted in so much pain. However, they also provided the greatest learning lessons going forward. For over five years, I had reflected upon this. I remember thinking to myself that the next woman I connected with I would give the world and all the love I possess. When it came to raising children, I just wanted to give my kids everything I longed for growing up. I wanted to teach them the right way to live, help them feel proud and confident in who they are, and love them unconditionally. But I was scared I might not get this opportunity.

As odd as it is to say, or for others to understand, coming home was not easy. That doesn't mean I wasn't grateful, but I was also scared. I had so much work to do in order to rebuild my life. I was living in a trailer on my aunt and uncle's property with no money, no assets, no career, no wife or kids. I knew what I wanted, and I knew if I didn't pursue that vision with the same determination I pursued my goals in prison—like my life depended on it—that I would regret it for the rest of my life. But where should I start? I was facing a conflict that I believe persists in most people's lives: Do I pursue my vision and follow my heart into the unknown or settle for security and the assurance a mediocre life offers?

It would have been easy to come home and settle. For most people, sobriety and a consistent paycheck would have been enough. I had five years of sobriety and the opportunity to work with my uncle and establish a safe and dependable career and the means to support myself. It was all right there for me. However, taking that route would have killed me inside. I'm not saying that would have been a horrible life; it's just not what I wanted in my heart. I was around the same people I'd grown up with in the same environment, yet I was different. And I just knew that I had to take action. I could never turn away from my innermost dreams and desires ever again.

Over the years, I'd written all those letters about what I wanted to do with my life. Every phone call would end with me passionately expressing aspirations, visions, and desires for my future. I meditated and visualized what life could be like living out my dreams. I had created these visions from a prison cell and brought them to life over time with constant care and attention. I had proven to myself who I was and what I could accomplish when I set my mind to it. Now was the time to show people, to show the world, to show myself who I was and what I was truly capable of.

I had been afraid of coming home and failing to give my all, that the learning lessons and transformative experience I'd had in prison would help me improve my life, but I'd still hold back and play it safe. Now, it seemed that fear was coming true. Working for my uncle's company each day felt like I was losing a grip on my dreams. I had built so much momentum while in prison, but now I felt off-kilter. My routines were different, my surroundings had changed, and I felt a loss of control over my life. I was so connected to my vision and purpose when I had time to reflect upon it while in prison. In there, time is in abundance. Getting out and jumping right into the faster passing life of society was a challenge. On the surface, to family and friends, I appeared as jovial as one could expect just coming home from prison. But deep down, I was afflicted, and it was concerning me.

Despite the changes I'd made over my five years in prison, I hadn't had the opportunity to allow others—or myself—to see that person yet. This was my struggle, a challenge only I could fully understand. I had to do something. I had to act. I remember feeling that way and thinking about what to do or how to take action toward my dreams. Where to start? Here I am living in a trailer on my family's property with minimal resources and connections. I didn't know how I would get started, but I had to find a way. That was the bottom line. I had to. Again, it was as if my life depended on it!

One morning, I woke up determined to break free of the internal struggle that had consumed me. I went running far back in the canyon at sunrise. It was a challenging run consisting of steep hills, and during that run, something shifted in me. I tapped into that same reservoir of inner strength and determination I'd found in prison on my long runs in the scorching desert heat. Something clicked. I felt something that was missing those first weeks back. All the fear, doubt, and anxiety I was experiencing started to melt away. I felt a surge of confidence and belief swell inside of me. At that moment, I knew I was back. I hadn't lost my spark; I wasn't daunted by the challenge. I had merely been adapting, and now I was eager to thrive. As a result of all the unknowns of my situation, I had allowed the resulting fear to consume my thoughts and emotions. This is the same fear and anxiety that would have derailed me in the past. So many people allow that energy to dictate the way they live their lives. I couldn't allow that to happen to me again, and I would do whatever it took to persevere.

After that breakthrough, I started to feel more and more comfortable in my new environment with each passing day. I started going on four-hour bike rides into the wilderness with my Uncle Mark. I was working, spending time with family, and going to Alcoholics Anonymous every day. Now, I was finally establishing a routine that allowed me to start building momentum slowly but surely.

The next step was deciding whether I would pursue a career in counseling or the fitness industry. Either I was going back to school to pursue my master's degree in psychology or I would start working at a gym and eventually create my own health and fitness company. I knew my passion was working with others, but I was indecisive about the best way to do that. I started networking and reaching out to anyone I could think of who could provide me an opportunity to move in the right direction.

One day, I contacted an old friend I'd gone to high school with who was working as a personal trainer back in my hometown. We spoke about my experience in prison briefly, and then discussed my background in fitness and working with others. He was surprised at how knowledgeable I'd become in regard to nutrition and sports medicine through my personal studies. When I told him I'd trained other inmates in prison and felt confident working with others, he took me seriously. I expressed to him how sincerely I wanted to help people and start making an impact on our community and people's lives. He offered me an opportunity as a personal trainer and told me that if I got certified, he would hire me part-time and set me up with my first few clients at the gym he trained out of. I was so excited. This was it, this was the opportunity I'd been waiting for!

OVERCOMING ADVERSITY

It's amazing how the universe has challenged me every step of the way. Anytime I felt a breakthrough emerging or an opportunity was presented to me, it seemed as though an equally daunting situation or obstacle would appear as well. I was being tested to see how badly I truly wanted to manifest my vision and live the life I dreamed of. Just when I had found that opportunity I'd been waiting for, adversity hit me hard once again.

My cousin invited me to go snowboarding one weekend. In prison I'd looked forward to getting out in nature so much. I missed the natural beauty of our world tremendously. Five years of looking at stainless steel and cement will numb your senses. When I got home, I immediately sought to be out in nature as often as possible. I was grateful and excited about the opportunity to go snowboarding and immerse myself in the brisk mountain air. We took a day trip and boarded all day long. I was exhausted by the last run of the day, and as we came down the mountain, I came through a tree line that had exposed rock. I tried my best to maneuver through the rocks, but I was tripped by the last boulder and flew headfirst, crashing into another rock just below the surface. I was stunned and found myself keeled over with pain shooting through my arm; the pain in my shoulder was excruciating. Only one hundred yards from the bottom on the last run of the day, and I had wrecked my shoulder. I couldn't believe this had happened.

For three days after, I iced my arm hoping it would heal. However, I decided to go to the hospital when I still couldn't lift it to eye level on the fourth day. The X-rays revealed what I was hoping to ignore. I had broken my scapula in half. The doctor's expression was grim as he revealed the news and told me that I would potentially have a limited range of motion in my arm after the break healed. The doctor warned me that it would be problematic with my active lifestyle and likely never be the same. Those were devastating words to hear. Just when I was starting to gain momentum, I faced a major setback.

I never accepted the doctor's words as a possibility, and in addition to the physical therapy they provided, I immediately started to rehab my shoulder in the weight room. It wasn't long before I was lifting weights again, and I gained back full range of motion as my shoulder healed faster than anticipated. More damaging than the pain I endured through that process was the loss of momentum. I couldn't work, and my plan to save money and move back to Santa Barbara to start my new career in the fitness industry appeared to be over before it ever began. I was at a standstill for a week or two trying to figure out what to do. Every day that passed where I wasn't in full pursuit of my vision and the opportunities at my fingertips felt like eternity. However, just like my experience with the doctor and those limitations he placed upon me, I wouldn't allow this to stop me from taking massive action.

With ample time on my hands, I focused on getting my certification in personal training and fitness coaching. The process typically took anywhere from three to six months to get certified. The courses were extensive and there was a lengthy textbook to read. The requirements included the completion of ten short quizzes, numerous essays, and a final exam. Each chapter in the textbook covered various topics pertaining to sports medicine, nutrition, and exercise science. When I was in prison, I always asked my family to send in books and material relevant to health and fitness. I had read every book in the prison library related to health, and I was educated on all the material required to pass my quizzes and exam before I even left prison. I had been preparing for this moment years in advance. I had an intuitive feeling that the time I spent training other inmates and my due diligence in regard to education would pay off tenfold upon my return.

I was able to get certified in two weeks. I spent countless hours each day writing essays and completing the coursework until it was done. I hardly read the textbook because I had already ingrained this information into memory. I knew the science and terminology verbatim. My time in prison was paying off in more ways than I can describe. That was such a rewarding feeling for me, coming home and seeing how my efforts while incarcerated were already helping me move forward toward the life I had dreamed of living for all those years. This was just the beginning, a glimpse of how I chose to spend each hour and day in prison could positively impact my life going forward. The lessons I learned were universal, and the foundation I'd built through my daily actions was sound. At that moment, I couldn't have been more excited and more grateful.

I called my friend and told him I was ready to start immediately. Now I just had to figure out the logistics of where I would live, how to make ends meet, and my transportation to and from work. I was eager but unsure as to how I could make everything happen quickly enough.

The ability to turn any situation into a positive one working for you as opposed to a negative one working against you is life-changing, and I had mastered it while incarcerated. Prison was my metaphor for life. I was able to turn a seemingly devastating situation into the opportunity of a lifetime. I would draw from that experience time and time again throughout my life. Even more than that, the things I did habitually while incarcerated and the changes I made to myself would impact my life forever. That mentality and approach to life became who I was and I was reminded of its benefits repeatedly upon my return home. I could have easily fallen into a depression or given up on my dreams with the amount of adversity I experienced early on. It was the way I chose to live every day of my life behind bars that gave me the strength and courage to fight through the challenges I faced and continue to follow my heart when I left.

A week after I broke my shoulder, there was a massive fire that engulfed our surrounding area. The fire raged for weeks, burning hundreds of homes and threatening thousands of others. We were forced to evacuate as my uncle's property was in jeopardy of burning. It's an understatement to say that it was a stressful time for my family and the local communities. We all had to stick together in those trying times and everything else in life was put on hold.

We were forced to evacuate immediately. The next day, we received reports that the fire was burning down homes on my uncle's street. We went up there to check on his property and see how bad the conditions were. From the road, all we could see was smoke and we had no idea if his house was still intact. I'll never forget standing at the base of his long driveway getting ready to run through the smoke and see what lay beyond. It felt like scenes I'd seen on the news, with the smoke covering everything in sight and the fire crews spraying down the hillside, doing their best to contain the blaze. A family friend and I decided to go check on my uncle's home. We sprinted through the blanket of smoke to the house and were relieved to see it still standing, unscathed. I jumped on the roof with the hose and turned it on to keep everything soaked just in case. As I did this, I remember looking up to see the home across the street engulfed in flames. The entire canyon was ablaze and the fire was moving fast. We frantically ran around doing the best we could to keep the grounds soaked in water and turn on any outdoor water spigots we could find. The flames were burning all around us and it was a terrifying sight. We got out of there as the surrounding wildlife was burning to the ground and smoke reduced our visibility to nothing. It appeared my uncle's home was going to burn down. There was nothing else we could do, and we were forced to evacuate down the canyon back into town. We waited all night to get reports about the property and, around midnight, my uncle received the call. While multiple houses on his street had been lost, miraculously his home had survived. We all breathed a sigh of relief and could sleep that night knowing his property had survived the inferno.

We ended up staying at an Airbnb for the next couple weeks while fire crews cleaned up the aftermath. All the power lines had to be replaced, and it would be weeks before we could return home. I can't imagine what my aunt and uncle were going through. As if this wasn't enough, a torrential rainstorm came passing through and caused severe mudslides and flooding. It was horrific. There were fatalities and the freeway was shut down going both directions. For everyone involved this was a very stressful and tumultuous time.

I was grateful my family members and I were safe. Many people lost their homes, lost everything. Reports were coming in of people who lost their lives, and it was a somber time for our community. In the coming weeks, things slowly started to return to normal as the threat of wildfires and mudslides dissipated. However, the damage had been done and it was severe. I found myself in limbo, unable to work, and stuck in this high-stress environment. The freeways were closed, and I had no way to get to Santa Barbara. This had all transpired only days prior to me starting my new position at the gym. I knew I had to take action. I couldn't just sit around for the next month and wait for the freeway to open and things to go back to normal. I had to make something happen. I was so close to a breakthrough, I could feel it.

I started thinking of ways to pivot and overcome this adversity. I had an idea, but it seemed far-fetched. My first month home, a good friend of mine had taken me flying over the Pacific Ocean in a single-engine Cessna. It was his way of welcoming me back. It was the first time I'd ever flown in a plane, and we planned to go flying together again soon.

I decided to reach out to him a week after the fires and see if he still had access to the plane. Turned out, due to the freeway being shut down, he had been flying down to the county I was staying in to pick up his boss and fly him in to work every day. I asked him if there was any room for me and explained my predicament. He didn't hesitate. This was it! Time to take action.

I met my friend the following morning at the small airport and rode to Santa Barbara in his plane. I had no idea where I was going to live, how I would make ends meet, or what was in store for me. I just knew it was time to do something. I had a job waiting for me that represented hope and possibility for the future, the future I'd aspired to live and the dreams I'd envisioned for so long.

One of the most exhilarating feelings in life is when you face your fears and the uncertainty that comes with a change in pursuit of what you feel in your heart. Despite all the unknowns, my decision to pursue my vision and go all in every step of the way was empowering. When we act in alignment with who we are deep down within and take the actions in life we've always wanted to take—despite fear despite adversity—something magical transpires within.

Even though I didn't have any details ironed out for when I got to Santa Barbara, I never felt worried. I was overcome with anticipation and excitement. I knew that the longer I stayed on my aunt and uncle's property, the more difficult it would be to achieve my goals. It had only been three months since I'd returned home from prison and so much had already taken place. However, this was it. This is what I'd been dreaming of all along and it was finally happening.

During our flight, my friend and I were talking about my plans once we got into town. I told him I wasn't sure where I was going to stay and my first priority was to meet with the owner of the gym I'd be training out of. He casually looked over at me and said, "Hey, my dad might have an extra room for rent." From that moment on, the pieces started to fall into place. As they appeared, I managed to fit them together. That was how it worked. It almost felt like everything had been planned out beforehand, but at this point, I was merely following my heart. There was no alternative plan. This was it!

When we got into Santa Barbara, my friend drove me to the gym where I'd train my clients. I met with the owner and my new boss, the friend from high school who'd been a fitness trainer for nearly a decade by then. He informed me that I'd start the next day at 5 a.m. After that, we drove to my friend's dad's place and within an hour I'd secured my room. I literally gave him all my money. Now I had a place to live and a month of rent paid. The next thing was to figure out how I was going to get around town. I had no car, and I wasn't sure what I was going to do, but I knew my uncle's mechanic lived in town and always had cars for sale. Before I left my uncle had told me it would be worth a shot to see if he had any old or used cars available. I called him up and he said he had three cars I could check out. I had no money but went to check them out anyway. There was one car my uncle's mechanic was willing to let me use temporarily or until I could pay him in the coming weeks. It was an older Honda Civic that he was fixing up. It had been in an accident, and the entire rear end was smashed in. When I say it was ugly, that's an understatement. Nevertheless, I had transportation and that's what I needed. It makes me laugh thinking about how I would park that car around the corner from the gym because I didn't want anyone to see me driving it. This was my humble beginning and, more than anything, I felt extremely grateful for the way everything was unfolding.

I was pursuing my dream and it was invigorating. There was no turning back. Within twenty-four hours, I had a new career, a new place to stay, and a car. Another fateful day where so much changed for me. Despite the chaos of raging fires and deadly mudslides, my broken shoulder, and the logistics of making it all work, I had managed to find a way. All the pieces were coming together because of my determination and the help I received from my family and friends. Every step of the way I had help. It is amazing what takes place when you follow your heart and don't hold back. My entire life, I had limited my potential because I let fear dictate my actions and never went all in to pursue what I truly wanted. This time was different. I was different, the energy was different, and the way life was unfolding before my eyes mirrored it. This was only the beginning, and I could feel it.

Now, instead of waking up at 4 a.m. to train myself in a prison cell, I would wake up at 4 a.m. to train my clients in the gym. I had been working with others for years and although the environment was different, the same underlying principles were evident. It didn't matter whether I was incarcerated or working in an upscale gym, my ability to connect with and understand my clients is what allowed me to help them. I was often asked when I was in prison and even upon my return if I was worried about what people would think of me being an ex-convict. It was always in the back of my head, but it didn't bother me. I was intent on showing everyone who I was and what I represented through my daily actions.

Because I was innocent of the crime I was incarcerated for, I wasn't self-conscious about being in prison. If anything, it was the opposite. I had an experience few could fathom. I looked at it as an asset, and I felt I could see or understand things about life in ways others couldn't. I would draw from my prison experience time and time again. I felt as though I could help others understand what I learned through my transformative experience and teach them by sharing my story and being transparent about my past. This had an impact on how I carried myself and my willingness to take action.

Also, I wasn't connecting with people in regards to just fitness. It was deeper than that; it was the void people felt within and the loss of motivation or excitement about life they couldn't figure out. I had felt that for many years, and in prison, I was able to discover the cure. When I realized this was the major affliction people were facing, the same one I had just overcome, I knew I was meant to serve on a bigger scale.

The way I was able to assimilate back into the community and connect with my clients uplifted me tremendously. I was set on continuing to improve myself and help those around me as best I could. However, not long after getting my first opportunity as a fitness trainer, I once again started to feel that something was lacking. Again, something was off. This was a very crucial moment for me because I'd always ignored my intuition in the past. I would find reasons to play it safe or make excuses that would prevent me from continuing to pursue what I felt in my heart. This was a theme that had played out my entire life. Now, it was as if the same lessons I learned in prison and all the same challenges I faced were being reproduced in my current situation. It was the perpetual battle fought within, facing our fears in order to realize our dreams. Every day we have a choice as to what voice we listen to and that decision drastically impacts our life outcomes.

FOLLOW YOUR HEART

By the time I was out of prison for a year, I felt a calling, a longing that I couldn't ignore. I was immensely grateful for the opportunity I had been given by the fitness trainer who hired me, but I knew I could do more, that I could connect with and help more people than I was reaching in the gym. Furthermore, I wanted to pursue my own creative ideas and my unique vision. I decided to leave that location to start my own company. It was definitely a risk, but I couldn't ignore my unyielding desire to create something of my own. The day I left I felt energized, invigorated. It was akin to what I experienced on that plane ride into town a year prior or when I signed up for my college courses in prison—nerves infused with pure inspiration and excitement, created by the unknown.

As soon as I left to start my health and fitness company, I experienced a surge of energy that had been suppressed. I was onto something, and I learned another valuable lesson that still influences the way I live. I must constantly strive to learn and grow to improve my circumstances. I must always follow my heart and allow that intuition to guide me even when fear and uncertainty try to stop me. This is a mentality and way of life that ensures we are fulfilling our potential and challenging ourselves to become the person we envision deep down inside. When I tap into that energy on a daily, monthly, and yearly basis, I am in complete harmony. Every day is full of excitement because I'm pursuing exactly what I feel within my heart. The feeling is incomparable. Then, when it's not there we know it as well. We feel the void or longing we may not be able to express, but the feeling never subsides.

Any moment that feeling fades or I feel some lacking in my life, I know I'm missing something. That's when my years of introspection become so valuable. That's when I pause and put everything on hold to reflect upon the truth and uncover what I may be overlooking or missing, once again returning to the same practice I mastered while sitting for hours in my cell alone lost in thought. This is the secret to keeping this miraculous energy within alive. I know I must continuously pursue my vision with every ounce of energy I possess. I must never hold back or limit myself; I must always follow the righteous energy and desire in my heart and continue to share it with the world. This was only the beginning.

Slowing down consistently and giving pause will allow your true thoughts and feelings to rise to the surface so you can be aware of them. The next step is to act upon those deep desires. Otherwise, we will feel irritable and anxious and long for something we can't even describe or understand. This is the major affliction most people face today. "I want more for my life, but I don't know what it is or how to attain it." Most people don't know they have all the answers, all they must do is uncover them within. The more I did so and the more action I took, the more my dreams started to come to life.

There was so much excitement in the air at that time in my life. The energy, the mystery, the journey—it was remarkable. I was giving my all to every moment, adventures with my cousins exploring the wilderness, watching my brother fighting MMA in Las Vegas, shark fishing out at the channel islands off the coast of Santa Barbara, skydiving on my thirtieth birthday with my brother and sister, running my first marathon, competing in triathlons, training for the Ironman, getting certified as a fitness trainer, becoming an entrepreneur, and pursuing my vision down to the minute detail. I was giving my all to life and soaking up every precious moment.

Physical challenges became a focal point of my growth at this time. It was my way to remind myself that I would never quit or give up, even in the most adverse situations. I could then continue to channel that confidence and belief in myself into everything I did in life. My newest challenge was to run the longest distance I ever had. I ran thirty-two miles up the coast, staring at the majestic Pacific Ocean as tears of pure joy streamed down my face. This was how I expressed my gratitude for life and my second chance at living. I knew no other way. I wanted to push my body to the limit to challenge myself but also to show others what is possible. People were intrigued by my attitude and the energy I was emitting. It was something uncommon, and people would tell me it was rejuvenating to be around.

When I came home I couldn't believe how many people were living their lives devoid of that excitement and inspiration. Everyone appeared bored and just going through the motions in their lives. I remembered what that felt like, a lack of conviction and purpose in our day-to-day lives. Eventually, that could progress, as it had for me at one time, into a perpetual state of imprisonment within our own minds. I was intent to share my story in the hopes it could inspire others and help them to see and understand this better. Maybe one thing I said or did could help someone who needed a sign of hope. Maybe through my actions and the way I lived my life, I could show people what was possible when we follow our heart and pursue that intuition every day. I had to share it; it was my responsibility.

People started to reach out to me on social media. Everyone knew I had been in prison, so when they saw me complete an Ironman event or the way I was living my life in general, I immediately got their attention. Wasn't this guy in prison? How is he living his life like this? I didn't feel like I was doing anything extraordinary. I was just pursuing the vision of myself and my life I longed for. I was living in accordance with what I felt in my heart, and it showed in the way I spoke and behaved. Others could see and recognize this. We all want that. We all want to live fully without fear and doubt holding us back.

I quickly realized that through such physical feats I could not only pique others' interest in what I was doing but it could also inspire them to push themselves as well. I started getting messages from people about the changes I'd made and how I was living my life.

They would tell me how I inspired them to start running again or to tackle some challenge in their life they'd been procrastinating. It was amazing to receive those messages. People were taken aback by how I'd changed in such a positive way while incarcerated. At first, they were somewhat shocked by how I was living my life and how happy I appeared. But I think that, when they saw the way I was living, they realized that maybe they were unconsciously holding back in their own lives. If I could come home from prison and make these changes, then they could too! I would get these inquisitive messages like "Dude, what are you on?" or "Wow, it's inspiring to see how you're living your life. How did you turn everything around?"

LOVE, FAMILY, & FULFILLMENT

I look back on that first year out with a smile on my face and pure joy in my heart. I have immense gratitude for

PRISON OF YOUR OWN

how everything unfolded since that fateful day I was arrested. It's not always the way I wanted or exactly how I imagined, but it's always exactly as it should be. To think that all the moments I've described and everything I experienced in prison and upon my return started as mere images attached to powerful emotions. My life has come alive before my very eyes and I still pause to this day in wonderment and profound gratitude for this miraculous journey. Everything is unfolding before my very eyes, and I'm here just observing it all as it does. Soaking up every precious moment, not wanting to blink because I don't want to miss anything. I am so in love with this life and I always longed to share this love with a family of my own.

When I came home, I was still trying to figure out how I would fit back into society, how other people would perceive me, what my relationships would be like, and so many other challenges. I had never dated or been in a relationship as the transformed person I was now. I had so many questions and concerns about dating and finding the right person. All my previous relationships had centered around partying and drinking. I was daunted initially, scared that no one would understand my sobriety and how it was literally life or death for me. I was worried I wouldn't find the love and connection I longed for with someone who could not only understand why I was the way I was and what I had been through but would support me and share my values as well. I spent many nights tossing and turning, playing out scenarios in my head.

When I came back home, it was as if my wife and I were magnetic, constantly drawn to one another. At first, I would see her out at breakfast or around town, but I never stopped and talked with her. It had been six years since I'd seen her last or spoken to her. However, when I first caught a glimpse of her again after all that time, I fell in love immediately.

Jessica and I have known each other since elementary school. She doesn't remember, but we were in fourth grade together. I have a faint memory of looking over and seeing the little girl sitting next to me in class, shy and quiet with big glasses that covered her face. It's unbelievable to think that, at that moment, I was sitting next to my future wife, the future mother of my children, my best friend, and my soulmate. Life is so amazing; it's so miraculous and unpredictable how it mysteriously unfolds as we try to make sense of it.

We shared mutual acquaintances growing up and knew of each other, but never connected until after high school. When we did finally spend time together, I fell in love with her. In fact, I've always been drawn to her and have never felt that way about anyone else in my life. However, at the age of twenty-three, I was a much different person and by no means ready to take care of anyone else because I couldn't even care for myself. I couldn't be the person she deserved and needed then. It wasn't the right timing. Nevertheless, that time we did spend together before my arrest sparked something between us that never faded, despite the miles and years that soon separated us.

When we reconnected shortly after I came home, it was easy to fall in love with her again. This time was different though. I was different. She was different, and together something magical was created. I've never felt so much love for another person as I do my wife. She makes me a better man and has helped me in more ways than I can describe. What was truly amazing was the timing of it all. While I was away in prison working on myself, she was growing as a person too. By the time I returned home, our values and our desires for the future were perfectly aligned. It just fell into place. We're truly made for each other, and when our love converged as it did, we were mesmerized. Through all my lonely nights in prison trying to picture what things would be like, I never imagined it would turn out the way it has. The first year we reconnected was magical, rivaling the most romantic movie. The love was infectious.

We quickly started to spend all our free time together, and before long, I moved out of the room I'd been renting and into her apartment. It was almost instantly that we both knew this was it. I'd heard stories of people saying, "I knew she was the one." That was exactly what I was experiencing, and my heart was full. I've never felt so much love for another person as I do my wife. All the precious moments and adventures we experienced together early on, the love and passion we share, the values and family-centered mentality show me we were destined to be together. She is the love of my life and my soulmate.

Jessica has been by my side every step of the way since we reunited. She gave me everything I needed at a time when I needed it most. Late at night, she was the one I would vent to about wanting to start my own company. From the very beginning, she and I connected on so many levels, and she would always listen and hear me out when I needed someone to talk to. The support she gives me empowers me to continue pursuing my dream and my visions every day. I can feel her unconditional love and support when I share my innermost feelings and desires, and she always tells me to go for it and that she believes in me and what I'm doing. She was actually the one who convinced me to stop waiting and to start writing this book.

When I was broke and struggling to grow my business early on, she paid for my ticket to compete in the Ironman. She knew how important it was to me. When I started training for it, she always took care of me when I came home exhausted after a five- or six-hour training session. When I participated in my first Ironman event, it was actually a half Ironman, we went to Santa Cruz, California, together and for the entire six hours I was out suffering, she was tracking my location and cheering me on from the sideline when I passed by. There are countless examples of her believing in me and pushing me to go after the things I desire in my heart. She knows I have a unique way I live my life, but she loves and understands me and why I'm this way.

Not only did I find the love of my life in that first year back home, but I was blessed with my son as well. Mason was eight years old the first time he remembers meeting me. Coming into his life at such an impressionable age has been one of the greatest gifts, challenges, and opportunities of my life. I am deeply moved when I think how my presence in his life could and will positively impact his future. In turn, he keeps me young and continues to inspire me to be at my best every day. I want nothing more than to infuse him with all the love and all the learning lessons I've experienced in my lifetime to help him pursue his own dreams and to believe in himself every step of the way.

That first year was a busy one. I found my soulmate, became a father, started my own business, and completed the Ironman. Just like that, I had the family I'd always wanted. All the visions and desires I held onto behind the prison walls were coming to life before my eyes. It was truly magical. On top of all that, I was able to form an amazing connection with Jessica's parents. Their love and support have been tremendous and getting to spend time and bond with them has been special for me. Ernie and Laura have shown me unconditional love from the day we met, and that has had a deep and powerful impact on me, more so than they could ever know. They are exceptional people. I deeply respect their values and way of life.

It was at this time that Jessica and I received the joyful news that she was pregnant. It was Christmas time, and after we found out, we walked down State Street in Santa Barbara as the Christmas parade passed by. I was in a daze, overcome by a radiant energy that enveloped me. I had spent so many of those lonely nights in prison crying out to God and the universe, asking for help and guidance, and wondering if I would ever have a family and children, and just a little over a year from the day I paroled, I had everything I could have dreamed of and more.

My journey has been wondrous so far, and as I write these words, I'm still in awe. The journey beckons me onward still, and I cherish every step I take.

Jessica and I decided to get married before my daughter, Scarlett, was born. I had wanted to give my wife a big extravagant wedding, but that wasn't possible then. I proposed to her on my birthday and we didn't waste any time, marrying two days later. Just like everything else in my life, we didn't hold back and just went for it. Saying my vows and looking into my wife's eyes filled me with love that radiated throughout my body. Two days after I proposed, I had my wife. Scarlett was going to be born in less than a month—and the magic of it all had me captivated.

And then, Scarlett was born. Any parent knows the unforgettable joy and emotion of holding their child for the first time. It's incredible to think of the instantaneous love you feel in that moment. Being with Jessica as she displayed indescribable strength in labor and then rejoicing with our baby was transformative. We felt so deeply connected and time stood still. Seeing Mason hold his sister for the first time added another level of depth to all of the emotions. He's an amazing big brother, full of so much love. These are the memories and moments in time I cherish.

From the day I paroled, I haven't wavered in pursuit of all that I value and desire. The most amazing existence is when we follow our heart constantly and never turn away from that intuition or allow fear and self-doubt to prevent us from doing what we love. I was done with talking myself out of things I truly wanted. I would never again allow fear to dictate the way I live my life. I would never again create an internal prison that I couldn't escape.

Finding self-love and peace within has transformed me completely. I've been given life when I previously felt dead inside. This second chance has afforded me an opportunity to do everything I always wanted but never pursued. I want nothing more than to share my experience with others in the hope that they can somehow relate to or connect with my story. I want nothing more than to see others thrive and excel in their lives. For anyone suffering or afflicted as I once was, I want them to know that there is still hope and change is possible no matter how devastating your situation is or how many times you've tried and failed. I am living proof that this is possible. Think of where I started. I changed—and you can too. I promise.

FINAL THOUGHTS FROM THE AUTHOR

I started writing this book, thanks to the extra push from my wife Jessica, at the very beginning of COVID- 19 and the quarantine. I could have found a million excuses to put it off but I knew I had to get my message out. This was a dream of mine I first entertained while in a prison cell and now it has come to fruition. I hope my message has opened your eyes and connected with you in a way that will positively impact your life. I understand It's not easy to make these changes but the reward is more fulfilling than you ever could imagine.

If you feel my story and the message I shared could help or inspire others to make positive changes in their lives I would ask that you please recommend my book to them. I would be so grateful. Furthermore if you could take the time to leave a review on Amazon I would greatly appreciate it and I look forward to personally reading all the reviews and feedback from everyone who read my book. Your support in this means the world to me. It is my mission to reach as many people as I can who feel lost or hopeless as I once was to show them that despite our past struggles we can persevere and lead meaningful and fulfilling lives.

One month prior to publishing this book my son Preston Michael Crane was born. He fought hard to get into this world and my family and I have been rejoicing in the miracle of life since his birth. Only weeks after welcoming Preston into this world I lost my father. His passing was devastating for my family and me as it came unexpected. We are never ready for the death of our loved ones no matter how much we think we are. R.I.P Stephen Crane, your spirit and memory live on forever in the lives you touched while you were with us.

I share this with you to illustrate how the same duality has been evident within my life and continues to be since the very beginning. It's despair and joy; heartache and love, fear and fulfillment. It's that same energy, good and evil, that I describe experiencing in my life or in prison that will always be a part of us. Within you is the same energy and only YOU get to decide where it gets placed. You can create any outcome you want in life, good or bad, it is YOU who creates your reality through the decisions you make and the person you create with those choices. Who are you breathing life into? The person you truly aspire to be deep in your heart or the person you have settled for?

Lightning Source UK Ltd.
Milton Keynes UK
UKHW022015190421
382278UK00003B/644